Business social media is the new cold call.

JEFFREY GITOMER

Social media is not just freedom of speech.

Social media is freedom of thought and freedom of expression.

JEFFREY GITOMER

Social BOOM!

How to Master Business Social Media

to Brand Yourself, Sell Yourself, Sell Your Product, Dominate
Your Industry Market, Save Your Butt, Rake in the Cash,
and Grind Your Competition into the Dirt – by the
Global Authority on Sales, Attitude, Trust, and Loyalty

JEFFREY GITOMER

FT Press

FINANCIAL TIMES

Jeffrey Gitomer's Social BOOM!

Copyright © 2011 by Jeffrey Gitomer. All rights reserved.

© 2011 Pearson Education, Inc. Publishing as FT Press
Upper Saddle River, New Jersey 07458.
Vice President and Editor-in-Chief: Tim Moore.

To order additional copies of this book, contact your local bookseller or call Jeffrey's friendly office at 704/333-1112.

The author may be contacted at the following address:
BuyGitomer
310 Arlington Ave., Loft 329
Charlotte, NC 28203
Phone: 704/333-1112 Fax: 704/333-1011
Email: salesman@gitomer.com
Websites: www.gitomer.com, www.trainone.com

Creative Director: Jessica McDougall
Pagesetting: Michael Wolff
Proofreading: Brad Baker and Claudia Cano
Cover design: Josh Gitomer

Printed in the United States by Edwards Brothers.

ISBN-13: 978-0-13-268605-1

First Printing, March 2011

Library of Congress Cataloging-in-Publication Data available upon request.

The Opportunity of Business Social Media.

Social media has become a phenomenon beyond words. Hundreds of millions of people all over the world have joined the party. In a millisecond, millions of people can know everything about everything and everyone.

You knew it couldn't be long before business got involved. Small business, big business, your business.

I'm 65-years-young. I've seen a lot of opportunities come and go. I have also seen the complete evolution of the computer, and the complete evolution of the Internet. But never have I seen, or could I have imagined, an opportunity so great as business social media. And the best part is, it's just beginning.

Now is your time to take full advantage of this low-cost (often no-cost), global, and local opportunity.

When companies like Procter & Gamble, Dell, Apple, IBM, Microsoft, Zappos, and Amazon dive head first into the process, you can be certain there is plenty of opportunity and plenty of room for you to do the same.

BUSINESS SOCIAL MEDIA REQUIRES AN INVESTMENT: Your time.

You must be willing to allocate an hour a day to build your network. When you do, and do it right, the rewards will be beyond your ability to measure. You will reconnect with business associates and you'll attract people and prospective customers to connect with you a thousand times faster and 10 thousand times better than making the 100-year-old cold call.

Business social media is the new cold call.

You'll make sales, you'll create loyal customers, and you will profit from your ability to expose yourself, your thoughts, your experiences, your interactions, and your value to your market around the corner, and your market around the world.

CAUTION: After you begin to see results, you'll curse yourself for not starting sooner. Turn that energy into action. Business social media is still young. There is still plenty of time. Commit to involve, decide to do it with value, intend to stick at it until you win, and reap the rewards both in reputation and in profit.

Get ready to ride the social media wave. It's a big one. Perhaps the biggest ever.

NOTE: I'm not writing this book alone. *Far from it.* I have enlisted the wisdom of others. Specifically: Sally Hogshead, Mitch Joel, Richard Brasser, Joe Soto, Noah Rickun, Mike O'Neil and Lori Ruff, Sandy Carter, Mark Schaefer, Chris Hamilton, Julien Smith, Andy Sernovitz, and Shar Govindan. I want to acknowledge them and thank them.

The world-class leader and expert of business social media has yet to emerge. Certainly it is not me. BUT I am proving to be quite successful at the process, and that's why I am sharing my strategies and what I believe to be true with you.

This is Not a Book.

Okay, okay, this *is* a book. BUT... *Social BOOM!* is also a "how to" and "what to" implement for and into your LinkedIn, Facebook, Twitter, and YouTube presence to develop a total business social media game plan.

This is a step-by-step, insight-by-insight guide that looks at the four main social media platforms in a new way – from big picture to implementable ideas and strategies that will build your attraction, your engagement, and your connections with valuable business customers, prospects, and contacts.

Social BOOM! reveals elements that create social attraction and business attraction by describing all aspects of building and executing a total market outreach. Each of these elements will be outlined in a way that makes understanding how your blog, email magazine (e-zine), personal website, articles, speeches, and other acts of value create energy and attraction back to your business social media outlets.

Social BOOM! inspires you to build your brand, your Google ranking, and your reputation as a person of value and a business of value.

KEY OPPORTUNITY: Create your own Social BOOM! by attracting customers and building your personal and business brand.

KEY UNDERSTANDING: LinkedIn, Facebook, Twitter, and YouTube are not options. They must ALL be used or BOOM! will never happen, much less meet your expectations.

KEY INGREDIENT: Your hard work and time allocation of ONE HOUR A DAY, *once you get your presence set up.*

What's So Social About Social Media? How Social Are You?

It started like a small bunch of rustling leaves. A little Facebook here and there – a blog or two. And then the wind picked up. LinkedIn, Twitter, YouTube. Growing from a windstorm to a firestorm, social media in now a tornado running wild over the Internet plains.

How social are you?
How serious are you about social media?

REALITY: You can't ignore it. Hundreds of millions of people are involved so far, and it's just a few years old.

> I tried to ignore it for a while, but it soon became apparent that this was the new, new wave – about two years ago I became a player.

I admit I have an edge.

I have a lot of readers and followers who are interested in what I have to say and want to know what my immediate thinking is. That's two of the advantages of social media. It is immediate and it is informative.

It's also fun! That's why Facebook and YouTube are worth BILLIONS.

The major networks in social media are growing quickly:

- Social networking for the growing and grown set is Facebook – worth billions.

- To get connected and network with businesspeople, it's LinkedIn – worth billions.

- If you want to say a few words, 140 characters sent to thousands in a second, it's Twitter – worth billions.

- For videos, it's YouTube – worth billions.

- For posting photos, it's Flickr – worth billions.

- And for that private message, there's texting – it's easy for me – I have an iPhone (priceless).

And that is just a partial picture. There's more…

- For individual expressions, there are blogs – where people you attract can subscribe to and link to your other social media pages.

- For chronologging it's Wikipedia – worth billions.

- And of course, there are your personal website and business website. Priceless.

All of these media are, or try to be, socially engaging – sticky if you will. All of them are, or try to be, passed on to others – viral if you will. Better stated, if you tweet, are you good enough or bad enough to be retweeted?

HERE'S THE GOOD NEWS: Everything you do in social media is documented on Google. And those documentations affect your ranking in a positive way.

I have made a serious commitment to "socialize" by exposing more of my personal self, and my business self, through social media. I maintain my value-based philosophy, but with business social media, I can personalize it, and humanize it, to a point that others are attracted to it, benefit from it, and want to pass it on to others.

I am business social and viral at the same time.

So, what does this mean to you?
What's the opportunity to you and for you?
Why should you get involved?

Social media is an opportunity, a new frontier, a space in cyberspace that gives you an individual place to play, builds awareness of you and for you, brands yourself, and from which you can potentially profit.

You have to ask yourself …

Where's the beef?

Where's the fun?

What's the value? Both to others and yourself.

And how – if desired – do you monetize it?

UNFORTUNATE NEWS: Unless you're one of the few people in an ownership or founding position of these social media, your monetizing opportunities are at the moment limited – in spite of various claims by "experts."

So here's what I recommend to get going and get positioned, so that your opportunity – either in social, business, fun, or money – can be realized:

- **Sign on.**

- **Establish an account on each of the major sites.**

- **Post something.**

- **Tweet something.**

- **Connect with someone.**

- **Do it yourself.**

- **Do it every day.**

And learn by updating as much as you can on your own.

Social media is fluid – it moves and changes daily. It's text, audio, photo, and video. It's every media and it's every second. It's current and it's constant.

Ever see a section of a website labeled "latest news," and when you click it, the last update is from 2004? Not good.

The Internet is instant. Social media is instant. And you have to be ready to participate consistently, and in a meaningful way, if you want to win.

Please don't wait.

Contents

LINKEDIN BOOM!

TWITTER BOOM!

YOUTUBE BOOM!

THE GLUE!

SOCIAL BOOM!

BOOM OPPORTUNITY!

The Social Media BOOM Is Here and You're a Bust!

Every time I'm in front of an audience I ask two questions:

1. **How many of you have some social media involvement? (Almost everyone raises their hands.)**

2. **How many of you wish you were better at it? (Almost everyone raises their hands.)**

Keep in mind that these responses are from a (supposedly) sophisticated group of people.

They all have smartphones; most of them get Facebook updates on their phones, but for one reason or another they have chosen not to enter the world of *business* social media. Many are on LinkedIn and have a few connections, almost none of them tweet, and even fewer have their own YouTube channel.

REALITY: Some HUGE companies have gone all out in social media, whereas others have their heads buried in the sand or are playing ME TOO, because they woke up one morning and found their competition gaining ground through a prominent and active social media presence. Still others are claiming "regulations" are keeping them from engaging.

Here are a few examples of big companies taking BIG advantage of business social media:

- **Starbucks asks for customers' opinions and solicits customers' ideas. (Where do you think the idea for that little green splash-stopper stick came from?)**

- **Burger King continues to let customers "have it their way" online with information and coupons.**

- **IBM utilizes every aspect of social media and has plans to double its effort in 2011 by trusting and encouraging its employees to become involved on a personal-business level with customers.**

- **Proctor & Gamble is all about Facebook and substitutes TV ads for social media presence. (WOW!)**

- **Ford uses social media as a PR communication device and consumer sounding board and feedback opportunity.**

- **Comcast tweets individualized customer service help messages.**

- **Zappos (as if they weren't customer service dominant enough) tweets their service response, and as a result receives THOUSANDS of positive retweets.**

All these companies, B2B or B2C, emphasize the same word in their philosophy and their outreach: COMMUNITY.

They all recognize that their customers have a voice, and, by listening and responding to them, they're discovering benefit and profit.

These are NOT isolated examples – they are typical examples of how big companies are using the power of social media to inform, communicate, serve, and sell.

How are you doing? What's your "community" strategy? Who are you listening to? Who are you responding to?

Or are you still answering your phone and "serving me better" with nine options? Pathetic.

Here are 6.5 TOUGH questions designed to make you think, plan, and act:

1. **What are you doing about the social media opportunity?**

2. **How are you attracting customers and prospects?**

3. **What's your value message beyond product offerings?**

4. **How are you engaging customers and prospects?**

5. **How are you connecting with the people you engage?**

6. **What's your social media doubling plan?**

6.5. **What policies, trust issues, and lawyers are holding you back? Get rid of them!**

Those are painful questions that need answering.

REALITY: And while you sit around strategizing and legalizing a plan, your competition is laughing at you, hoping you'll delay even more.

I tweeted this quote last night: "The more you hold your people back from using social media at work, the more your competition will kick your ass."

TWEET POWER: Less than one hour after it hit the Internet, more than 50 people had retweeted it, and more than 100,000 were exposed to the message. And me. FOR FREE.

People have made the following statements, or asked me the following questions, over and over:

- How can I use social media to attract new customers?
- Isn't social media for kids?
- I have never tweeted.
- I tried social media and didn't get any results.
- My boss won't let us use Facebook at work.

And this is my response:

Individuals (like you) can safely set up their own value-based, value-messaging BUSINESS Facebook page INSIDE the parameters of whatever guidelines their business has. And they can do the same with LinkedIn, Twitter, and YouTube.

PROBLEM: It requires hard work and consistent posting.

OPPORTUNITY: You can be recognized by your customers, prospects, vendors, industry, and community as a leader and value provider.

MAJOR CLUE: Start today!

Business social media is a huge NOW opportunity. Your ability to attract people to your presence is enhanced by the relationships of value that you have established over the tenure of your business career.

JEFFREY GITOMER

The Social Revolution and Your Evolution.

The social revolution has changed the way you sell and serve forever. Only problem is, most salespeople have no idea of that – YET!

As business social media evolves and matures, all salespeople, executives, and entrepreneurs will expose themselves for who they are and who they aren't... WAY BEFORE a sales call or sales meeting of any kind takes place.

Think about the impact of that…

- I'm gonna Google YOU.
- I'm gonna Facebook YOU.
- I'm gonna find you on LinkedIn.
- I'm gonna look you up on Twitter.
- I'm gonna search you on YouTube.

And you can't stop me.

I'm gonna find out EXACTLY who you are – the same way you're trying to find out stuff about me.

Two years ago, it wouldn't have happened that way. At least on the social media side. Maybe five years ago for Google.

Today, ALL systems of selling are preceded, and sometimes precluded, by your online reputation. Before I ever call you, before you ever call me, before you ever meet with me – I already know everything I need to about you.

Or I can look you up in 10 seconds WHILE you are on the phone or waiting to enter my office.

Here are the NEW standards by which you'll be evaluated, granted appointment time, decided upon, measured, branded, and talked about (whew!):

Your Google presence and ranking

Your online reputation

Your business social media presence

Your personal website (present or absent)

Your blog (present or absent)

Your Facebook presence

Your LinkedIn connections and recommendations

Your Twitter followers and tweets

Your YouTube presence

Feel a little overwhelmed? That's because you've been asleep at the wheel waiting for the economy to "rebound." That's because you think the Internet is about your company, not you. That's because you're waiting for your attorneys to figure out a "corporate plan" for social media.

Wake up and smell the Internet, Sparky!

Here are a few things you should do, and can do – that if you don't do, you'll be "doo doo:"

- **Look at what your competition and their people are doing on the Internet.** Study their online presence and their social media presence.

- **Talk to your customers IN DEPTH.** Find out what they would consider valuable to know, and make a plan to deliver that information, whether it pertains to your sales or not. HINT: If you provide valuable information, it directly pertains to your relationship, and their loyalty to you.

- **Allocate more of your time to learning what you don't know about "online."** At least an hour a day. If you're behind by your competition's standards, that's one issue; but if you're behind by your customer's needs, that's THE issue. If you don't know what to do, start studying, and start getting involved.

- **Set achievable goals and measure your results.** Start with LinkedIn. Get 200 connections and expand your network from there. Create a few testimonial videos on YouTube that feature your customers talking about how great you are.

- **Communicate value messages, not product offerings.** The purpose of your online presence (especially on social media) is not to sell, it's to attract people who want to buy.

- **Seek professional help. BUT BEWARE.** Get personal references BEFORE you spend a dime. There are a lot of people who can help you. There are many more who CLAIM they can help you, but cannot.

- **Waiting is more expensive than starting.** Whatever your budget for online and/or social media presence is, it's cheap compared to doing nothing while others pass you by.

Social media is not going away. My bet is that your business social media presence is lacking. And there is not one good reason for it, other than your foresight is limited by your insight.

It is my hope that the strategies and ideas in this book can help you kick-start what you're doing online – especially your social media participation – so you'll have no regrets (also known as hindsight).

Free Git✗Bit... Want to know three tips to live without regret? Go to http://www.gitomer.com and enter the word REGRET in the GitBit box.

Social Media – The New Cold Call. Wanna Play?

People are quite polarized about the social media craze.

It's an Internet tug-of-war between the believers and the nonbelievers. And one by one, the believers (the users) are dragging the nonbelievers (the nonusers) across the line.

Which one are you?
Still making cold calls?

REALITY: Millions of businesses have social media logos on the front page of their website. How many businesses have your logo on their front page? Who wants to connect to your people? OUCH!

Here are 5.5 major business implications – to help you convert from cold calling to attracting new customers – that are afforded through this new online phenomena:

1. Facebook. You have found your old high school or college friends – or better – they found you. That's your "social" page. Do you have a business page where people can "Like" you? A business page is the way to give value and attract new friends and customers. If you post something of VALUE about your market, your industry, or your product, you could actually ATTRACT prospects.

REALITY BYTES: Facebook was recently valued at $9.5 billion. It was founded by a couple of 24-year-olds that have changed the Internet forever in less than six years. Rock the house.

2. LinkedIn. All business, all opportunity, all connections. But it's just a giant leads club until you figure out what your value proposition is, and how to deliver it. The key right now is to build a base of connections and consistently deliver value messages to attract more.

3. Twitter. The newest of these social media, it's gibberish to some, money to others, and mystery to most. I tweet one value message every day. I tweet my own thoughts and words. And I recommend you do the same. If your tweets hit home, someone will tell someone else, thereby increasing your exposure and attraction.

4. YouTube. If it's a video world, why are you without your HD Flip video camera? As you know from MTV, video killed the radio star. I have a dedicated YouTube channel where I post sales tips and random rants about attitude, trust, loyalty and other business value points. How are *you* taking advantage of YouTube? Where are your customer video testimonials when you need them?

5. Flickr. Photos to post and photos to find. In a 10-year space of time, one-hour photo shops have gone from boom to bust. Digital images and photo printers have killed the radio star. Look at photos of others to learn about them; post pictures of family so they can learn about you. Attach your photos to emails. Use them in presentation slides. Post them on Facebook. It's fun, and it's a great way to build understanding and relationships.

5.5 is YOU. The most important element of social media *is you*. It's all about what you write, what you do, what you post, what you tweet, what you shoot, what you record, how you participate, and your dedication to make your personal message and your personal brand attractive.

There are key words to consider as you try to build your social media world: connections, attract, video, value, consistent, fan, relevance, write, allocate, monetize.

HERE'S THE BIG SECRET: How you position and promote yourself in the NON-social media world is critical to your success in the social media world.

Your writing, your website, your blog, your e-zine, your personal brand, your reputation in your marketplace, your perceived value in your marketplace, and your Google rank are elements of attraction that affect your social media status – and surely your success.

And then there are the charlatans, and those trying to take unfair advantage of others. Like anything else in business there will always be a small percentage of idiots and zealots doing the wrong thing. Ignore them. Don't let the actions of a few spoil your outlook to advance and grow.

REALITY: The cold call has been part of the selling world for more than 100 years. And it's over. Technology, guards, gatekeepers, voicemail, and the overall sophistication of buyers and executives, have forever changed that landscape. This is GREAT news!

GET SOCIAL: By implementing the free opportunities afforded on Facebook, Twitter, YouTube, Flickr and ESPECIALLY LinkedIn, you have an incredible opportunity to attract and connect with prospective buyers.

There are billions of dollars of new business being generated by making social media connections. How much of it will you get? Maybe you need to get a bit more serious about being a bit more social, and a bit more attractive.

Are You in the Social Media World? Or Standing on the Sidelines Waiting?

Social media has changed the world. Let me clarify that statement. Social media has changed YOUR world.

Whatever you're doing online, whether it's Facebooking, LinkedIning, tweeting, or YouTubing, social media has changed your way of communicating one-on-one, one-on-customer base, and one-to-the-world.

FACEBOOK IS THE EASIEST PHENOMENON TO UNDERSTAND. It has changed the way you communicate with your friends and your family, and has opened the freedom door to anyone that you come in contact with, either business or personal.

On Facebook, you have found old friends, schoolmates, and co-workers – and they have found you. In the same way, you can find customers and prospective customers – and they can find you.

Because of social media and the Internet, big companies no longer have a big advantage.

Anyone can create a news blog that can immediately attempt to compete with *The New York Times*. The music industry has been leveled by groups performing their own songs and selling them on iTunes, and groups are creating free videos on YouTube. They're doing it far more efficiently, at far less cost than records or CDs since they have been invented.

LINKEDIN HAS CREATED A NEW WAY TO COLD CALL AND A MUCH MORE SOPHISTICATED WAY FOR BUSINESSES TO CONNECT. You can go on LinkedIn and search by job title and find prospective customers at no cost. It's also the employment agency of the future.

TWITTER ENABLES YOU TO GAIN A FOLLOWING OF PEOPLE INTERESTED IN YOUR THOUGHTS, YOUR INFORMATION, OR THE INFORMATION OF OTHERS THAT THEY PERCEIVE AS VALUABLE.

YOUTUBE IS THE NEW MOVIE THEATER AND YOU HAVE ABOUT ONE BILLION VIDEOS TO CHOOSE FROM. Millions of new movies are added every day. If you have heard the expression, "To the cloud," YouTube currently occupies half of heaven.

People interviewing for a job completely expose themselves through their presence on Facebook, LinkedIn, Twitter, and YouTube the same way a company is exposed in social media. And yet there are people who discount social media, avoid it, and even bad mouth it. Those people are fools and you know some of them.

REALITY: Social media and business social media have created new sales, new marketing, new exposure, new branding, new communication, new networking, and new business opportunities – the likes of which have never been seen or known before.

The revolution is just starting, and most businesses, business people, business executives, and salespeople are still social media inept.

NOTE WELL: There are few things or actions, and there are few people or circumstances that can change the rules of the game. Social media has changed all four.

People, circumstances, things, and actions have all been changed forever as a result of posting, tweeting, linking, and connecting. And the people that have taken advantage of it have changed their outreach in a way that has all their traditional competitors shaking in their boots.

Think about your social media place as you plan your marketing outreach for the next 10 years, and ask yourself these questions:

1. **What's my current position in my marketplace?**

2. **How do my customers perceive me?**

3. **Can my customers access my company 24/7 to leave comments and tell stories?**

4. **Do I really know what my competition is thinking and saying?**

5. **How attractive am I to my customers?**

6. **What's my value proposition that favors my customers and how do I let them know it, day after day, without simply repeating it?**

I have only been actively involved in social media for three years. This year I am going all out to attract, engage, and connect. I have hired a consulting firm to help me. I have three people on staff posting events, monitoring my accounts, and helping me.

AUTHENTICITY: I do my own tweets, either dictate or post my updates on Facebook, and I am active (accepting invitations, and responding or corresponding) on LinkedIn. I believe that staying personally involved keeps my message true to my philosophy, and helps me learn.

There is an unspoken strategy for businesses to employ and that strategy focuses around the word *value*. The more you offer, the more attractive you will become. The less you offer, the more anonymous you will remain.

JEFFREY GITOMER

Converting Personal Social Media to Business Social Media.

How are you using and profiting from social media?

HERE'S THE PROBABLE ANSWER: You're using it but not profiting from it.

And that's because...

- Your Facebook page has photos of Sunday's picnic, 15 comments from close friends and relatives, and nothing about business.

- You have a Twitter account that tells your audience of 75 you're in your pajamas and going to bed. (Even more insulting that you call your followers "tweeps" or "tweeple.")

- Your LinkedIn account (if you even have one) has under 100 connections, and none of them have ever received a value message from you.

- You do not have your own YouTube channel.

Ouch.

REALITY CHECK: It's time for you to draw the line and the distinction between personal social media and business social media.

There is an easy way, and a no-cost way, to create attraction and connections from business social media.

I'm challenging you to take advantage of it. Starting now.

Here are two things you can do TODAY:

1. Create a business Facebook page that your customers, prospects, and fans can "Like." A page for your business enables you to create an opportunity for dialogue with your customers and prospects. It also challenges you to create value messages, post videos, and offer tips and ideas that will help your customers and prospects build their business – and the result is you can gain a following.

Take a look at my business page on Facebook, and note how I post on a daily basis, and how I create links back to my website so that the people who like my page can continue to perceive me as a value provider and a resource. While you're there, take a few moments to read the comments that I get in response to my value offerings. It's humbling, flattering, and creating a revenue stream. You can do the same.

I would gamble that every one of your customers and prospects is already actively involved with Facebook, but likely only on a personal or social level. You can easily find them and ask them to like your page.

CAUTION: Your business Facebook page requires work, constant updating, and response. You zero out your credibility if you post only once a month. My rule of thumb is a minimum of three times a week. It's most interesting to me that even when I don't post, one of my fans will post something for me or about me: a quote, a thank you, an idea, or a story. To me it's not just a post, it's a report card – people taking time from their day to interact with me and share their gratitude, their question, or their idea. *How many people like you?*

2. Twitter is an anomaly and mandatory. Most people fritter away their Twitter opportunity. They're either saying nothing, or soliciting sales. In my first year on Twitter, I tweeted approximately 180 times, and from that I gained more than 15,000 followers.

Yes, I have an advantage being a published author and speaker, but I took advantage of my advantage.

I'm now one year and four months into Twitter, and I just posted my 218th tweet yesterday. "Resilience is not what happens to you. It's how you react to, respond to, and recover from what happens to you." I had more than 100 retweets that enabled me to pass the 20,000 mark of followers. If I suggest for people to do something in my tweet, it's so that they can gain more valuable information without a solicitation.

The value of Twitter has not yet been realized. But with 175 million users, there has got to be a few dollars in there floating around someplace. Take a look at my tweets, so that you can see the example of how I offer value.

And note that when I post a quote, it's my own. I'm not telling you what Benjamin Franklin or Albert Einstein (both brilliant people) said. I don't want to quote someone else; I want to quote myself.

One of my early Twitter quotes was, "If you want to be relevant on Twitter, tweet something relevant." It got hundreds of retweets.

What are you doing on Twitter? How are you taking advantage of 175 million people with 140 characters each day?

Social Media or BUSINESS Social Media? You Choose.

Of all the business social media options, I believe LinkedIn is the most valid and the most valuable. But it is not the ONLY.

To master business social media, it takes a successful combination of your business Facebook page, your Twitter account, your LinkedIn account, and your YouTube channel.

LinkedIn enables you to find people that can possibly do business with you, be a valuable contact, and (more important) enables people to find you.

Most of the salespeople that use LinkedIn are trying to find leads and/or beg for some kind of connection. This strategy is the least useful, but it's better than a cold call.

LinkedIn has a wealth of CEOs and other C-level people in its network, and millions of entrepreneurs (yes, millions) who own their own business and can make a final decision.

LinkedIn is the new cold call. Instead of calling a gatekeeper and fishing for information on one possible decision maker, you can now advance search on LinkedIn and find exactly who you're looking for BEFORE you make the call. You can discover who is connected to your connections and find people by job descriptions and job titles.

Your job, as a master of business social media, is to attract them, not beg them. Your job is not to find them. Your success will come from letting them find you.

Of my thousands of connections on LinkedIn, I have asked less than 100 people to link with me. The others asked me to link with them. That should be your goal.

Here's a total business social networking strategy:

REGISTER WWW.YOURNAME.COM. If your name is taken, put the words "I am," or "the great," or "the one and only" in front of your name. If all of them are available, buy all four. If your last name is available, buy that, too.

ESTABLISH A SIMPLE ONE-PAGE WEBSITE. On it, post your philosophy of how you treat customers. In a short period of time, this will help give you a ranking (probably a number-one ranking) on Google so that people can easily find you.

THEN CREATE A BLOG. (Wordpress, Typepad, or Blogger offer free or low-cost options.)

THEN CREATE YOUR BUSINESS FACEBOOK PAGE, YOUR LINKEDIN ACCOUNT, YOUR TWITTER ACCOUNT, AND YOUR YOUTUBE CHANNEL. Make sure they're all in your name or contain your name. This gives you even more Googlejuice, and will give you a half-a-dozen listings or more on Google.

The key is to make yourself visible on the Internet – through your website, by blogging, and via value-based use of social media.

I also recommend that you go to http://www.aceofsales.com and establish an account. It's only $20 per month and it can enable you to access Facebook, LinkedIn, and Twitter from the homepage with one click. It will also enable you to create and send out your own e-zine.

Read more about Ace of Sales on page 180.

Now that you have the big picture, here's what to do:

1. Tweet a value message every day. Just one. Something that your customers and your prospects would consider valuable.

2. Blog one paragraph every day that includes your tweet. Something that others consider valuable. All you have to do is wake up in the morning and start writing.

3. Connect your social media accounts so that what you post on one appears on all of them.

4. Post events of importance on your business Facebook page. Especially post interactions with customers.

5. Now begin the invitation process. Start inviting everyone you know, and everyone you can think of, to join you on LinkedIn, "Like" you on Facebook, follow you on Twitter, and check out your YouTube videos. Make the invitation *a personal one*, not a standard one. Not everyone will honor your request. But when people start to receive valuable information from you on a regular basis, they will begin to tell others. People will comment on your Facebook page. They will retweet you. And they will proactively connect with you on LinkedIn.

NOTE: As you can see, the key to business social media is being business social proactive with a value message.

NOTE WELL: It will take you less time to write 100 words of value than it does to make 10 cold calls that you'll be hung up on, or 10 unsolicited emails that will get deleted.

5.5 What's YouTube got to do with it? Take a look at the Buy Gitomer channel on YouTube. I've taken 100 short value messages and videotaped them. If you take the paragraph that you blog each day and record it on your Flip video camera, then you can upload it to YouTube (in about one minute). Posting your content on YouTube enables people to see you and your passion in action, and to feel your commitment and your validity. It gives people an opportunity to get to know you, even if they've never met you. Keep in mind you don't need to have a million views on your YouTube videos to make them valuable; you need only a handful of executives and other decision makers to regularly look at your posted messages. Eventually they will click and buy from you.

NOTE WELL: I'm not telling you what TO DO. I'm telling you what I DO. I invite you to join me on each of these social media, to see what I do every day and learn how I'm beginning to monetize it – so you can do the same.

Free Git✗Bit... The true monetization opportunity of social media is still relatively unknown. If you'd like to know a few specific examples of how I've monetized my presence, go to http://www.gitomer.com and enter the word MONETIZE in the GitBit box.

9 Ways to Fascinate the Goldfish.

By Sally Hogshead

A hundred years ago, you didn't need to fascinate the goldfish.

Back then the average attention span was about 20 minutes long. (An estimated one minute for each year of age, up until age 20.) But then, a little thing called "The Internet" happened. Now we have messages coming at us from every direction: voice-mails and videos, emails and apps, updates and upgrades, tweets and retweets.

So how do our brains respond to all this stimulation? Turns out, we're learning to think differently. We think more quickly and get distracted more easily. The BBC has announced, "The addictive nature of web browsing can leave you with an attention span of nine seconds – the same as a goldfish."

Nine seconds! (That's just long enough to read one tweet.) *That's all we get before our customer's brain makes a decision to either stay focused or relocate to a new topic.*

In this distracted environment you must immediately spotlight your unique competitive advantage.

You have only an instant to communicate, convince, and convert.

In this nine-second world, the most fascinating messages triumph, the most fascinating salespeople triumph, and the most fascinating products and services do, too, because they earn a customer's attention.

What does all this mean for you?
You must learn how to sell to goldfish.

After you learn how to fascinate the goldfish, you win!

- **You win bigger budgets, better relationships, and greater admiration.**
- **You build stronger loyalty, bigger networks, and deeper trust.**
- **And, you can charge a higher price.**

If you fail to captivate your customer, you will lose. It's that simple. The goldfish will swim away to the next salesperson, the next ad, the next low price.

Today, it isn't enough just to have a better product. It's not enough to be the best if no one realizes you're there.

Wondering where to start?

In my book, FASCINATE, *I describe how to develop persuasive and influential messages. To build your own social media empire, here are nine ways to instantly begin to attract, convince, and retain the goldfish:*

1. HAVE THE BIGGEST BUDGET. OR BE THE MOST FASCINATING. PICK ONE. Your social media can be as boring as you want, under ONE condition: *You have a bigger marketing budget than anyone else in your category.*

If this is the case, you can afford enough advertising to just hammer it in, over and over, wham-wham-wham, until people remember.

That's what Fortune 100 companies like Kellogg's and AT&T and Microsoft do. They can afford to be un-fascinating.

Oh – what's that you say? You don't have a Fortune 100 budget? Well then. Until you do, avoid being pointless. You can't afford it.

To begin, work on the message itself.

2. MESSAGE FIRST. MEDIA SECOND. There's a lot of hoo-ha about all the different forms of social media: Twitter and Facebook, YouTube and LinkedIn. All of which are important.

BUT: *Before you even think about which form of media to use, you must first decide <u>what to say</u>.*

As you consider different platforms, remember: The message is not an afterthought. It's king. Emperor. World nuclear superpower. Don't "do" social media unless you actually have something to say.

Get your message right first, and the rest gets a whole lot easier. How to do this? Read on.

3. IDENTIFY WHAT ALREADY MAKES <u>YOU</u> FASCINATING. Yes, your company has the potential to be fascinating. The trick is to figure out exactly *what to say*, and *how* you can use that to attract customers.

Here's a quick version of an incredibly useful exercise I do with my Fortune 500 clients to help them uncover their brand's main points of fascination. I call them "Fascination Badges."

In advertising, we develop ONE key strategy.

But in social media, it's good to have an abundance of message points so that you can share fresh information to reinforce your main points and motivate consumers to engage in multiple ways.

The purpose of this Fascination Badges exercise is to develop a profusion of points that clearly distinguish you.

Brainstorm a list for each of the following points:

- **Product.** How you're different or better than the competition.

- **Core beliefs.** The values that guide you; what you stand for.

- **Actions.** The ways in which you "walk the walk".

- **Culture.** How you work, communicate, interact, play, promote.

- **Heritage.** The "back story" of how you became the best.

- **Benefits.** Why someone should buy from you or hire you.

- **Purpose.** The mission behind why your company exists.

Use the lists you come up with to create several messages that demonstrate what makes you different, better, and more fascinating than your competition.

You don't *always* want to talk about yourself, of course. It's also important to connect by sharing information and insight.

4. START WITH INFORMATION, AND THEN ADD INSIGHT. Ever sent a magazine article to a colleague, perhaps adding a Post-It note of personal commentary, as a way to bond over a problem or goal or interest that the two of you share? Sure. And you can build relationships through social media in exactly the same way. Sharing relevant and useful information (such as a news report or an emerging trend) conveys your investment in supporting your network, rather than just promoting yourself.

Now, ready to step it up a notch? Add *insight* to your message.

When you share info, go a step further to include your interpretation of the material, and the implications for your reader. Connect the dots.

It might go something like this: "Here's something on the horizon: ____, and here's what I believe it means for you and your business: _____."

Insight requires a little more effort and sophistication, but increases the relevance of your message – and of your brand. *Adding insight is adding value.* Otherwise, you're just spamming people.

You might not think of your marketing as spam. But if no one gets value out of your message, sorry, it's spam.

5. THINK IN VERBS. Successful social media messages don't just get attention – they drive behavior. They incite action. If people don't change their actions as a result of your message, that message failed.

To create messages that change behavior, *identify exactly what action you want people to take.* Rather than just making an announcement ("Now open Sundays" or "20% off!!!"), start thinking of messages in terms of how your message will:

- **Attract customers into your store**
- **Prove why you are the best choice**
- **Increase urgency for immediate sale**
- **Convince new prospects to switch to your product**
- **Recommit to being loyal (when they might otherwise move to a competitor)**

In social media – and in life – verbs are the foundation of success.

6. HIT HOT BUTTONS. Hot buttons are intensely charged issues that tap directly into a customer's decision to buy. Different customers have different hot buttons. Identify which hot button will most influence the purchase process, and then create messages around it.

Here are three potential hot buttons:

> **Fears:** What is your customer concerned could go wrong, and how can you prevent or solve this? (FedEx fear uses this hot button, charging a premium for "fear relief.")

> **Needs:** Identify what's *missing* or *unsolved* for your customers, on a practical level. Do they have a rational need (such as the need to spend less)? Or, an emotional need (such as feeling validated by a well-known brand name)? Find ways in which your business fulfills what's missing.

Hopes: Deep down, your customers hold certain aspirations (even if they won't admit it). They might want to feel smarter, more relaxed, or even get promoted as a result of buying your product. Although it's easy to identify your customers' rational needs, it takes some savvy to demonstrate you understand *what they aspire to become.*

All this isn't easy. Social media works because *you* make it work. And that takes work.

7. STOP MOANING THAT IT'S HARD. Yes, it's hard (especially at first). Agreed. Get on with it. Just start. How? *Write about something that fascinates you and why.* Press enter. BOOM. Done.

Social media isn't a one-time deal, like creating a logo, or designing a billboard. It's free, and it's incredibly effective – but it takes a regular commitment akin to brushing your teeth, part of your consistent repertoire.

When you first start building a network and establishing your point of view, you have to put energy into the process. But soon, the process gives energy to you as people start to respond, react, and (most of all) buy.

I recommend a blend of personal observation, questions, and your own thinking.

To help get you started, here's a batch of my most retweeted messages from the past month. Feel free to share any of these messages on social media – as your own:

> *You can be comfortable, or outstanding, but not both.*
>
> *Trust your gut. It's smarter than you.*

You are your most important client.

On Sunday evenings, do you prepare for Monday morning by gearing up with gusto? Or do you savor every last possible moment of weekend time?

My career advice: Forget what your business card says. You're an entrepreneur.

The McRib Sandwich: Yummy? Or culinary freak show?

8. STILL FEELING STUCK? TRY ONE OF THESE:

- **Go on a rant.** Or a rave. Or anything else you sincerely feel strongly about. A passionate voice vividly communicates what you believe in and why people should care.

- **Ask provocative questions (and interact with the resulting commentary).** Once, I posted on Facebook: "Would you rather work for a talented asshole, or a sweetheart hack?" There were so many comments and discussions on Facebook, Twitter, and my blog that it led to a two-part article in *Advertising Age*.

- **Predict what will happen next.** Or what you think should happen next.

- **Praise a company that's doing things differently and getting it right.** Maybe even praise your competitor.

- **Use social media in unexpectedly direct ways.** What if you use Twitter to cleverly woo a potential new client? Most people keep a close eye on any mention of their own usernames, and their company's account, so your tweet will automatically pop up on their alerts. You might say, "Reason #47 why @AcmeCo should hire us: We guarantee our work for twice as long as anyone else."

Personalize it even further by tweeting messages to individuals in the company. A cool, cheeky way to pique their interest.

- **State your "opinions of authority."** These strongly worded viewpoints are like a letter to the editor but relate to your customer. It must be a topic or sentiment that you can stand behind so confidently that it reflects your expertise. Your opinions of authority shouldn't be obvious; in fact, the more counterintuitive, the better. What do you believe with such conviction that you can authentically advise your customer with full confidence? And what if you make a short YouTube video or blog post about it?

So why aren't more people fascinating? Because it requires strategy, street smarts, cojones, and an understanding of human nature. It requires developing and expressing a distinct point of view.

It's easy to be boring. Anyone can do it. Your competition probably does it quite well.

9. STAND OUT OR DON'T BOTHER. (SERIOUSLY.) Are you willing to create ideas that irresistibly attract an audience of avid followers? Are you prepared to do the work necessary to inform and inspire your audience? Are you courageous enough to provoke and occasionally polarize? Are you unafraid to ask questions and change the way people think?

If not, don't waste your time and money on social media. Really.

The world doesn't need another tweet. It needs *you*. It needs your secret best practices, your offbeat observations, your old-fashioned advice, and your cutting-edge solutions.

The goal here is to create messages that are remembered and acted upon. But it all starts with being heard.

You will not win by being quiet.
In a nine-second world, you win by being heard.

Growing up with the last name Hogshead would give anyone an unconventional point of view. Today, Sally is on a mission to help companies create radical ideas and passionate action, expertly shaken and stirred with a tangy slap of inspiration.

An author, speaker, and internationally-recognized marketing expert, Sally works with world-class brands such as Coca-Cola, Nike, and Target, and frequently appears in national media including "The Today Show" and The New York Times.

Sally's latest book is FASCINATE: Your 7 Triggers to Persuasion and Captivation. *How does your own personal brand irresistibly captivate? Find out by taking Sally's F Score personality test at http://www.SallyHogshead.com/FScore*

Is Social Media Right for Every Business?

By Mitch Joel

A great man once said, "Do or do not, there is no try."

Fine, it wasn't a great man. It was a Muppet. But when Yoda said that now-classic line in *The Empire Strikes Back*, many a geek (myself included) nodded our heads as if it were the commonsense wisdom of the Dalai Lama.

In fact, the concept of "trying" something without having a true strategy or direct outcome in mind is becoming a much more sensible approach to the Digital Marketing channels.

This is especially true when it comes to the varied world of social media, where channels and platforms like Twitter and Facebook roam wild with Foursquare and Quora. One person's video of six dogs chasing a gazelle with 80 million views is equally layered against an audio podcast that focuses on the best burger joints in Montreal. (No joke, check out: The Montreal Burger Report at http://montrealburgers.blogspot.com/.)

Is there room for your business and brand in all of this random content? Of course there is!

One of the primary reasons that businesses struggle to understand the world of social media is that it's often compared to just one particular traditional media channel, instead of it being seen as a healthy ecosystem where a brick-and-mortar brand (and this includes both products and services with a business-to-consumer or business-to-business focus) can create and do things with content (text, images, audio, and video), across multiple areas, and with varying degrees of impact and audience.

That is the new reality, and it is always surprising to hear many social media pundits say that, "Social media isn't for everyone."

The explanation that follows implies that some companies simply don't have the wherewithal to get it done... and get it done well.

A lot of businesses don't have the bandwidth, budget, resources, people, experience, or the right attitude. It's as if everything has to align like a total lunar eclipse to get into this very complex media mix. That kind of back and forth is a huge misnomer.

It's usually done so that a company hires any one of these many consultants/speakers/gurus/experts/wizards to pay them to do the work.

The truth is that asking, "Is social media right for my company?" is a flawed question.

Instead ask yourself this, "Should my business be sharing who we are and what we do with the world?" What is your answer to that question? If it's not "Yes," feel free to close this book and whack yourself upside the head until you realize that the answer is and likely always will be, "Yes!"

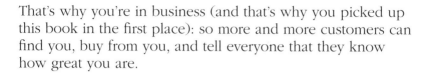

That's why you're in business (and that's why you picked up this book in the first place): so more and more customers can find you, buy from you, and tell everyone that they know how great you are.

This flawed thinking that social media is not for everyone happens because many of these self-anointed experts focus on only two areas of social media:

1. **Whatever platform is most popular (like Facebook and Twitter).**

2. **The notion that social media is all about the "conversation" that is taking place online about you, your competitors, and/or the industry you serve.**

Those are both valid spaces to play in (and if you do everything that Jeffrey is telling you to do in this book, you'll get there), but they're not even close to the only ones, or the reason to get involved with social media in the first place.

What makes social media (or any other type of media) truly "social" is the ability to share. Whether that is done on an internal basis with your employees, or publicly (or both), sharing is the best place to start. Sharing is also a key pillar in building trust and credibility.

Share everything there is for people to know about you and your business – news, articles, white papers, your thoughts, etc. Share beyond your own hallowed digital walls (your website) and push that information into the channels where people who might be looking for what you have to offer.

That being said, make sure that all of the content on your website is just a click away for people to "Like" on Facebook, or "tweet" on Twitter, or email to a friend.

(You can learn more about how to do this and get a free widget to place on your website that will allow people to share your content right away at http://www.sharethis.com.)

While optimizing your site so it can be found on the search engines is still critically important, don't forget that YouTube is actually the second-largest search engine after Google. So if you're not producing a video blog, or posting video testimonials and your public speeches, you may not be reaching every potential customer that is looking for you.

While sharing gets things rolling, being findable is equally important. Every day, more and more people are now doing all kinds of searches and research within their online social networks. They're scanning the industry blogs and podcasts to see who is saying what about whom and making informed purchasing decisions based on the responses they get back.

> The more your business makes your content more findable – in text, images, audio, and video – the more findable you become... everywhere, but you have to be listening, too.

People frequently ask me if social media platforms like Twitter are a waste of time. As the President of a Digital Marketing agency with two offices and over 130 full-time employees, I can tell you bluntly that it's my job to know what people are saying about our brand, our clients, and the industry we serve.

It is also my job to be listening for new business opportunities and to close more sales. If people are asking for references to a digital marketing agency on Twitter (Facebook, LinkedIn, or wherever), it's incumbent on me to be there, and be responsive.

Yes, you can purchase social media monitoring tools to hear and capture everything. But you can also access some amazing free tools like Twitter Search (search.twitter.com), Google Alerts (www.google.com/alerts), and Google Blog Search (blogsearch.google.com). Start listening. Right now.

Once you begin to benefit from sharing, listening, and becoming more findable, you'll begin to see the many additional options and tools that are available.

From tools that can help you to better collaborate both internally and by leveraging the wisdom of your crowd to listening to the existing feedback and dialog surrounding your brand – all of this public content is there. It can help you better analyze your market position, what customers really think about you and your competitors, and – if you're listening close enough – it can even provide indications as to how you can improve, innovate, and close more sales.

What if you sell toilet paper? Is social media still right for your business?

Charmin released an iPhone app called "Sit or Squat" that allows you to locate, rate, comment on, and even add a clean public toilet. The feature-rich application also allows you to narrow your search to bathrooms that have a baby changing station (as one of many examples). This crowd-sourced initiative has been downloaded millions of times and – as someone who travels as frequently as I do – has a special place on the first homepage of my iPhone.

Charmin is enabling and empowering people like you and me to share with the intent of having a better bathroom experience (and the hopes that you'll consider buying Charmin toilet paper as you make your way through your grocer's aisle).

If Charmin can make social media work using toilet paper, what's got you all blocked up?

Here are five ways to start listening, sharing, and becoming more findable:

1. Open up. Beyond the ShareThis functionality, consider allowing anybody and everybody to be able to rate and comment on all of the products and services on your website.

2. Listen better. Set up a free account with Google Reader and start feeding into it RSS feeds for all of your key/ important terms (company, brands, key management people, competitors, industry, etc.).

3. Read more. Use Google Reader to also organize all of the key blogs and podcasts in your industry. By reading, listening, and following them, it will make you smarter and sharper. You'll you'll know what your competition is up to and be able to think of ways to beat them.

4. Listen even more. Use Twitter Search, Google Alerts, and Google Blog Search to hear what people are saying about you, your competitors, and your industry. Here's a tip: every search result will (usually) allow you to create an RSS feed. Do this and bring the feed into Google Reader. This way, you will have one area where every time anything is mentioned, you'll be able to see it in this one, unified, and easy-to-manage location.

5. Respond. Respond to everything. What is said about you. What is said about your industry. What is said about your competition. Become the de facto expert. Don't sell. Don't push. Be helpful. Be likeable. As my friend Hugh McGuire (LibriVox, iambik) likes to say, "Don't Blog to be known. Blog to be knowable." In this instance, respond to become knowable. If you are knowledgeable and helpful, people will buy from you.

Mitch Joel is President of Twist Image – an award-winning Digital Marketing and Communications agency. Marketing Magazine *dubbed him the "Rock Star of Digital Marketing" and called him, "One of North America's leading digital visionaries."*

In 2008, he was named one of the top 100 online marketers in the world and was awarded the highly prestigious Top 40 Under 40. Most recently, Mitch was named one of iMedia's 25 Internet Marketing Leaders and Innovators. His first book, Six Pixels of Separation *(published by Grand Central Publishing), named after his successful blog and podcast, is a business and marketing bestseller.*

For more info about Mitch, visit http://www.twistimage.com or follow him on Twitter at http://www.Twitter.com/mitchjoel.

The Secret Door:
8 Steps and You Are IN!

By Richard Brasser

One of the most common complaints I hear from salespeople is that big company executives are extremely difficult to connect with. One of the main reasons is that there are intentional barriers put in your way. I can almost guarantee you that most access points to the decision maker are well fortified with screeners, guards, high walls, and tar-filled moats. However, through the use of social channels, not only can you learn about your prospect, you can also connect with them directly and better yet, get a response.

Before diving into the best ways to utilize this "secret door," it is important to first understand why it exists and what motivations are keeping it open.

The rise of social communication via the web marked a significant change in the way that technology aligned and empowered our human instincts. It is the "human" part that makes this paradigm shift different and also the key that drives our motivations. Technology has been advancing at an amazing rate since the first computer started to blink its lights. All of a sudden we could perform tasks that were impossible before. We could do them faster, and highly complex things were made relatively simple.

Faster and easier was great, but it also came with a high likelihood of headaches. Nothing seems worse than when technology abandons us at a critical time without an easy fix. Regardless, it was worth the tradeoff.

Technology continued to develop and assist in our communication. Email, webex, faxes, conference calls, IP phone systems, and virtual offices were enabling us to work from anywhere.

This was GREAT! Kind of. We had flexibility and mobility, but we were getting more and more impersonal. We were losing human interactions and connections at an alarming rate, and came to find out that it wasn't the big things in life that helped us bond with someone, it was the little things. It was the delicate weave of personal and professional daily actions, insights, questions, and realizations that were the fabric of our relationships. We were losing those. And it felt empty.

At the same time and driven by the same need, a strange emphasis and value was starting to be put on "notoriety." Notice that I didn't say "fame." It wasn't the desire to be famous that people were yearning for. Sure it would be nice to win seven gold medals or win an Oscar, but this was more about just being noticed.

In a world that was becoming increasingly anonymous, people just wanted other people to say, "I see you and acknowledge that you are there."

This may seem overly dramatic, but pay attention and you will see it everywhere. Contestants on reality shows are not driven by the money (although I am sure they are ok with it). They are not driven by the need to show people their amazing abilities. In fact, they are not even concerned with being perceived in a good light. They are doing anything necessary to be NOTICED.

The new currency is quickly becoming "attention," and it is driving the majority of social media. Ask an 18-year-old whether she would rather have $50,000 or a YouTube video with a million views, and I'm sure you can guess the answer.

ENTER THE WORLD OF SOCIAL TECHNOLOGIES: These new tools tapped into both of these key drivers. They satisfied our need to connect in a very human way AND develop a network of "followers" or "fans" that think you are interesting. Facebook didn't rocket to its hundreds of million users in less than six years because it had a good product or offered a good value (although free is nice). It did it because it tapped into a deep-seeded human need and the world was insatiable.

So why should you care about any of this? Because understanding the underlying needs and desires is everything! The tools and technologies will certainly change. New companies are launching every day, offering slightly different versions of existing tools or entirely new services.

Base your strategy and knowledge on the underlying principles, and you will have a solid perspective to evaluate any change in the landscape. Additionally, understanding the motivations of your prospects' use of social media will help you navigate the use of your own social media and give you a clear understanding of what is going on.

Don't just take these tips and act on them without understanding why they work. Understand why they work, and you can begin to think up a lot more of your own and continue to create new strategies as the environments change and mature.

Remember, we are at the dawn of social communication. It has gained much momentum and attention, but it is a long way away from maturity. The entire industry reinvents itself every 90 days, and you need to be empowered to grow with it.

If we reflect on these motivators and start to look at the executives' use of social networking, it will start to make sense why these tools provide such an unobstructed tunnel to connect with them personally.

Here are three aspects of social networking that open the "secret door" and ensure that you will have the ability to connect directly with your prospect:

1. Social networking is a personal brand. Even for social media that's business focused, the entire social framework is built around people generating content and growing their network. They might be trying to promote their company's products or services, but they do it as real people. The general corporate voice just doesn't work well in social media. Why? Driver number one! It's the personality and unique insights that other people want to connect with, not the brand or product. The result of this is the executive managing and creating his own social network. Further result? Direct pipe into his world.

2. Social networking is a river. Social networking is a continuous conversation. It is difficult to outsource. Have you ever tried to have someone else talk on the phone for you while you were standing there? Eventually you just say, "Give me the phone." Remember, it is people connecting with people. If anyone gets the feeling that you are shouting one-directional messages out into the social networking world, you will be banished quickly. That kind of behavior is simply not tolerated. Therefore, not only are the executives managing their own accounts, they are constantly checking them for updates. This gives your messages a much better chance of being noticed. Compare this to email. It's probable that your prospect has five or six different email accounts. As you get closer and closer, they are probably screened by someone else before ever being forwarded to the direct account. Even if you get a direct email address, they probably get hundreds a day and find it easy to delete or ignore your attempt to connect. So why is social networking different? Driver number two! People gain nothing from responding to an email, but they build their network and gain notoriety by responding to a mention on the social networks.

3. Social networking is a fish bowl. The core DNA of public
social networks dictates that they are open and in plain view
for everyone to see. A good friend (and top executive at
Facebook) explained to me just how seriously this is taken
when he said that his leadership told him that "Facebook
would never build anything that was private!" It is always
dangerous to say "never" but understand that transparency and
openness is at the core of what drives social communication.
Therefore, you can trust that your prospects aren't hiding
behind a corporate firewall of anonymity; they are playing
out in the world in plain view. They are motivated to connect
and be on their absolute best behavior. It is similar to meeting
someone at an event. They will be quite courteous, polite, and
respectful…because that is how they want to be perceived
and because they know everyone is watching. Back at the
office they can ignore your call, cancel your sales presentation,
and not respond to emails because no one is watching. Social
networks enable you to connect with the BEST version of that
prospect, and that is a wonderful thing.

What an amazing little alternate universe where your same
prospects are polite, responsive, motivated to connect, and
willing to interact! Still think social networking is a waste of
time? I didn't think so.

As long as you understand how and why these drivers
work, you can create hundreds of your own examples and
be even more effective. Remember, BE AUTHENTIC! This is
not about taking advantage of people or manipulating them
into a conversation. This is about offering them real value
and being a real person. If you aren't willing to do that, then
don't bother. Nothing sticks out more than a self-serving
salesperson in the social media world. Be real, be yourself,
and be honest and the results will surely follow.

This is a real-life example of how I got a meeting with the CEO of a large and prestigious technology company by having him reach out and thank me. Sounds strange, right?

HERE'S HOW IT HAPPENED: I had respected him and his company for many years. I started following his messages on Twitter. I noticed that he had a 75% to 25% balance between work and personal. He liked being a professional thought leader in his space and was grateful when someone furthered that cause.

Every once in a while, he paid particular attention to certain topics or opinions and carried on longer conversations. Those messages seemed to be most important to him, and he was responsive to any feedback. I followed closely and found one opinion of his that I really liked and agreed with. I retweeted his message to my network with the addition of "great opinion by top thought leader."

You get the idea.

I also mentioned him on a couple following messages and gave him credit for starting the thought that I continued. A few days later, I received a message from him thanking me for my kind words. I responded and explained that I have been a fan of his for a while and would love to connect the next time I am in New York.

He said "no problem" and a few weeks later, we scheduled a meeting. All of this because he reached out and thanked me! Could this have been achieved through traditional communication channels? Probably not.

Wondering how to get started?

Let's take a look at eight professional steps for using social networking to get an audience with almost anyone you seek:

1. **FIND YOUR PROSPECTS.** What networks do they participate on? Where do they spend most of their time? Make a list and link it to their profile or add it to the contact information you have for them.

2. **FOLLOW THEM.** Don't just click to follow, and then ignore them. Really follow them.

3. **READ THEIR POSTS.** This might take a bit of time, but resist the urge to just jump in and start trying to communicate. Read their tweets or other posts for a while, and you will start to get a good feel for the subtleties of their communication. It is these subtleties that will prove to be the most important in the long run.

4. **COLLECT INFORMATION.** Setting up an ongoing search in Tweet Deck (or any other similar tool) for their Twitter name and their company is a good way to have a broad perspective of what is being said. The nature of the social network is that it is a large and complex hub and spoke system. Just focusing on one source might give you a skewed perception. Find as much as possible about what is being said.

5. **LISTEN.** Don't just hear, but really listen. Try to understand their perspective, their predispositions, their biases, and their style. At this point, it's much less about the individual messages and more about the ongoing conversation. Are they directive or passive, aggressive or accommodating, egotistical or humble? Knowing this is important when trying to understand their communication style.

6. **CONNECT** – If you have done the previous steps, you are ready to make the connection.

   Depending upon where they are spending the most time and how they are participating, your approach will vary quite dramatically, but here are a few general ideas to get started:

   A. Retweet some of their most impactful messages. Adding a few words of your own.

   B. Mention them in your tweets as having influenced you or helped you in your business life. Be honest and straightforward. They will see these messages. Almost everyone, no matter how big their following is, tunes in when their name is used.

   C. Tweet about their success, articles, press, and so on. Be a supporter and they will appreciate your efforts.

   D. Find relevant LinkedIn groups that they participate in and offer intelligent and original answers or comments. LinkedIn groups are a great way to quickly "have something in common" with your prospect. It is also likely that other similar prospects are in the same group, so pay attention to who the other group members are. If a group is not "open," then you can't contribute, but you can always reference the discussion in your updates from LinkedIn or Twitter.

   E. Start topics that are likely to engage your desired audience. You have the ability to start topics within a group or outside of a group. Be careful not to be too self-serving or make it feel like an ambush. People are wary of salespeople asking questions that they themselves are dying to answer. You have to be a bit more creative and smart with this one.

F. Answer questions that your prospects are asking. This is kind of a no-brainer, but make sure you have a useful and impressive answer.

7. **REACH OUT** – Direct message them or try to connect in a more meaningful way. On LinkedIn, you can ask someone else who is in their network to introduce you. On Twitter, you can send a direct message if they are following you as well. Use other communication channels and reference the social network where you noticed them. WORD OF CAUTION: Don't try to friend people on Facebook that you don't know or just have a business relationship with. You can "Like" their business Facebook page, but their personal Facebook is their more private world and unless you are invited, please respect them. Also, it is not recommended to connect on LinkedIn directly unless you know them. It is actually against the user guidelines to attempt to connect with someone you have never met. If you have never met them and can't find anyone to introduce you, their public profile is the only information that you should use. Be respectful and honest in your approach.

8. **ALIGN YOURSELF WITH THE PEOPLE THAT YOU KNOW THEY FOLLOW AND PAY ATTENTION TO.** If you have listened well to their updates, you will know who they respect and who they don't. Having a person that you both mutually respect can be a great common connection. Retweet or mention those people and your prospect will probably see those posts as well.

Generating sales is often a numbers game, and it's alluring to try and cast a wide net.

However, spending a little extra time getting to know the person beyond the target is well worth the effort. Truly understanding the human motivation and drivers for the explosion of social networking will pay huge dividends and enable you to easily navigate around most traditional barriers and find "the secret door" to success.

With more than 11 years of experience in the interactive media world, Richard Brasser has become one of the leading experts in social media and interactive marketing.

As an acclaimed speaker, author, and thought leader, Richard has been a speaker for the Inc. 500 conference, an "Entrepreneur Roadmap" board member for the Kauffman Foundation, and a member of the Social Media Task Force for NASDAQ.

Since founding The Targeted Group in 1999, Richard has helped some of the nation's leading brands create their social networking strategies and successful interactive media initiatives. Aiding in strategic marketing programs for companies such as SAP, Siemens, Citibank, Smith Barney, Avaya Nortel, GMAC, Pepsi, and RSM McGladrey, Richard has honed his understanding of how to create engagement and long-lasting value using social strategies.

You can follow him on Twitter at http://twitter.com/socmedia365.

FACEBOOK
BOOM!

The Difference Between Social Media and Business Social Media on Facebook.

Take a look at your Facebook profile page.

Do you see all kinds of pictures of you and your friends and your relatives? That doesn't seem too conducive to business. More like monkey business. Almost like a chat room for all your friends to see your life, and for you to see theirs.

And although it's mostly positive, some of it contains drama, and all of it is wide open.

Now, take some time and look at a few business social media pages. They're easy to find. All the large corporations have one. Look at those first, and then try to find some small business ones. Then look for your competitors, maybe even look for your own company. Take the time to research Facebook before you continue reading.

Now think of all your customers, your prospects, your vendors, your business contacts, and your business connections. What can you do to invite them, or should I say, entice them to like your business Facebook page?

HINT: The key word is value.

THE DEEPER EXPLANATION IS: Discover what would be valuable to them and what would entice them to join you and others to exchange information or glean information that would help them build their business with ideas and implementable actions.

And when they see enough examples from others, they might have the incentive to post stuff about themselves.

Facebook's "page" term is a misnomer. It should be a "community" where all of your customers, your prospective customers, and even your vendors would find you as the focal point for information dissemination.

It's not difficult, but it does take work and consistent response on your part. And that work will translate into a leadership position, a stellar reputation, and money if it's done right.

There is one Facebook page I would like to direct you to. Mine. Look at the examples that I'm giving, look at the responses that I offer, and look at the comments people make after they attend one of my seminars, read one of my books, or get my weekly e-zine.

HERE'S MY SECRET: The more I give, the more attractive I become, the more engagement I create, and the more connections I gain. It's certainly not a secret formula but it's a recipe of ingredients that will not cook on its own. You are the chef, you are the chief, and you are also the waiter.

Bon appétit!

Oh No, Not Facebook! AHHHHHHHHHHH!!!!

What's your company's social media policy?
Probably shortsighted.

Social media, or social networking – better defined by the larger players Facebook, LinkedIn, Twitter, and YouTube – has become more than a global phenomenon. When combined with your online presence and online outreach, it's a global business phenomenon and a revenue-generating phenomenon. If it's done right.

Many businesses are using social media.
Many businesses are not using social media.
Many businesses forbid social media.
Many businesses are still trying to figure out what to do.

Wake up and smell the retweets! Social media is not only here to stay, but the few that are heavily involved are (silently) also reaping the benefits.

Why silently? Because they don't want their (stupid, chicken, technophobic) competitors to wake up and get on the bandwagon, or should I say, brandwagon.

NOTICE TO THE SHORTSIGHTED MANAGEMENT THAT IS AFRAID TO LET THE NEW WORLD IN: I assume your healthcare package includes bloodletting.

REALITY: There's a huge trust factor at hand – you can't treat your salespeople like children and expect them to act like adults.

What your management is saying by restricting social media access is:

- We don't trust our people to do the right thing.

Management is also saying:

- This is how we want our young employees to perceive management.
- We want to create an opening for competition to steal our customers.
- We want to create an opening for competition to hire our disgruntled employees.
- We want to create an opening for a huge morale issue.
- We want to create a word-of-mouth issue about our low technology and trust.
- We want to create a perception to customers of our inferior technology.

And worst of all:

- We want to lose an unbelievable chance for feedback from customers.

Here's what management should be doing:

IDEA: Create a social media training program for what it is, how it works, and what to do to succeed.

BETTER IDEA: Seek professional help.

BEST IDEA: When you establish guidelines, tell employees what they CAN do, not what they can't do.

Here's a simple list of 3.5 things to do as you enter the social media world:

1. Model after others who are successful.

2. Create attraction through value and valuable information offered.

3. Offer value before asking for money.

3.5 Don't stick your big toe in the water. Dive in!

Need more reality?

- **There are 500 million people (and counting) on Facebook** – Who's your fan? Who likes you?

- **There are 65 million business people on LinkedIn** – What's your share of connections and leads?

- **There are 175 million people on Twitter** – How are you sending value messages to thousands of customers and prospects – for free?

- **There are millions of videos posted on YouTube every day** – Why aren't some of them yours?

- **There are millions of YouTube videos viewed every MINUTE** – Why aren't your customers viewing yours?

REALITY 1: The sales pressure is on for EVERY company in this country. Maintain volume, improve, survive, make profit, and hurry up. Go out and make more cold calls – generate more activity (whatever that means).

REALITY 2: Social media is the new cold call, and you are still dialing for dollars, or pounding the pavement? How about trying to keyboard for connections?

REALITY 2.5: Sales management and senior management better realize this, or they will begin to rot in their own ineptitude.

By coincidence, I'm in Kitchener, Ontario (Canada for the geographically challenged), to deliver a seminar to a group of tech people wanting to sell better and sell more – people who are not natural-born salespeople. How did they find me? Eh, on the Internet! Through my e-zine, my Facebook page, and my tweets.

Ask yourself...

> **How many people are finding me?**
>
> **Who's my fan?**
>
> **Who's following me?**
>
> **Who's retweeting me?**
>
> **Who's reaching out to connect with me?**

ANSWER: Not enough people!

And for those of you about to email me to tell me you've been cold calling for 20 years blah, blah, blah – go turn on your laptop. You're right. Cold calls do work.

One out of 100 times.

Free Git⋏Bit...I came across a piece I think will interest you. It's a chief marketing officer's view of what to do to be effective on each of the social media platforms. It's not gospel, but it's a perspective I think is worthwhile to read. To judge for yourself, go to http://www.gitomer.com and enter the word CMO in the GitBit box.

What Should I Tweet?
What Should I Post?
How Should I Link?

Most people don't know what to say on, what to do on, or what to do with social media. And it's a club with more than 700 million members.

There has gotta be an opportunity in there someplace.

HERE'S THE THOUGHT REALITY: Stop thinking of it as social media, and begin thinking of it as BUSINESS social media.

Immediately some clarity begins to creep in. You're already using LinkedIn as a business proposition. You're getting contacts, finding prospects, searching by company and title for qualified people to connect with (link with). You may even be job hunting or job upgrading.

Why not use Facebook, Twitter, and YouTube the same way?

Why not create daily/weekly/monthly value messages that your customers would find so interesting and informative that they would save them, print them, put them into action, and forward them to others?

Sounds way more powerful than cold calling and groping, grasping, begging, or manipulating your way to an appointment (that will most likely result in rejection) even if you use your fanciest, newest "closing technique."

Cold calling is such a cruel joke in this day and age.

TODAY'S REALITY: Do everything you can to use business social media to build brand, image, reputation, and perceived value with your customers and your business community.

YOUR CHALLENGE: Send messages that your customers perceive as valuable to them. Messages so valuable that they will tell others.

BUSINESS SOCIAL MEDIA REALITY: It's not about searching out someone on Facebook; it's about someone finding your business Facebook page and liking it. It's not about finding someone on LinkedIn; it's about them finding you and wanting to connect. It's not about tweeting; it's about being retweeted. It's not about posting a video on YouTube; it's about someone sending your video to someone else.

"But Jeffrey," you whine, *"How do I know what's most important or most valuable to MY customers?"*

THINK: What will help your customers produce more, profit more, understand what's new in the market, improve morale, improve attitude, and/or improve their life? Then write about it, tweet about it, and post on Facebook about it.

MAJOR CLUE: Many people tweet or post something someone else said. WRONG. It's not what somebody else says that is meaningful to your position as a person of value in business social media; it's what *you* say, what *you* think, what *you* have experienced, and what *you* believe to be true.

DO THIS: If you sell toilets, you have to talk about plumbing. If you sell insurance, you have to talk about protection, or peace of mind. If you sell clothing, you have to talk about fit and fashion. If you sell automobiles, you have to talk about vacations and auto safety. If you sell real estate, then you have to talk about building equity, home repair, and front yard safety.

BUSINESS SOCIAL MEDIA SELF-TEST:

- **Make a list of your last 10 Facebook postings.** How many people like your page? Do you even have a business page?

- **List the last 10 actions you took, or messages you sent, on LinkedIn.** Anyone join you or want to link as a result of them?

- **Make a list of your last 10 tweets.** Are they relevant to your business success? Did they help others in any way? How many got retweeted?

- **List the last 10 videos that you posted on your YouTube channel.** Are you posting value messages that your customers and prospects would watch, learn from, and think of you as a resource? Any video testimonials posted on your YouTube channel? (Short testimonial videos will help prospective customers buy and reinforce your own belief system.)

There are all kinds of books and seminars available on social media and business social media. I recommend reading as much as you can and attending as many as you can. And my biggest recommendation is: START NOW.

I am issuing the challenge. I am listing the opportunities. I am providing how-tos. The rest is up to you.

All business social media is interconnected.

You have to do ALL of them consistently to gain effective results. And you have to do all of them well if you expect to monetize your efforts.

JEFFREY GITOMER

Starting Your Own Business Facebook Page.

Here is a 5.5-part success formula:

1. Gather the email address of each one of your customer contacts. There may be three or four connections at one place. Then gather all your prospective customers whether you have spoken to them or not (email addresses and names). Then gather all your vendors, prime connections, and the CEO of every vendor you have. If there are end users involved in your sales chain, gather as many of them as well. How many names and email addresses do you have? Never think, "I don't have enough names." Even if you have only 50, and those people are loyal advocates of yours, you can begin to create your own business Facebook page.

2. Begin gathering valuable content that your customers would perceive as usable and profitable. Information that they would consider so valuable that they might forward it to somebody else. Gather lots of it. Think of it this way: Every paragraph that you have can be one day's post. Don't start your business page without at least 30 days of postings.

3. Have your business page designed graphically and strategically. Sometimes it pays to pay. If you seek out and hire credible, professional help in design AND strategy, you will get incredible results. Although the ability for graphic alteration within Facebook is limited, that doesn't mean you can't use what's available to its maximum power. How your page looks to others, and the value of what you post, creates the attraction power. How you link to other ports of "you" builds your following, your reputation, and your limelight.

4. Your Facebook page has to be a door that swings both ways.
People attracted in from value and people that can immediately
click out to find out more about you.

5. Use my page as a guideline. It's designed to make certain
that I have linkage to all other business social media and
all other forms of attraction. It even has a welcome video
that describes what the page does so that people have no
hesitancy to "Like" me.

**5.5 Sign up for Ace of Sales (www.aceofsales.com) to create the
coolest emails on the planet.** And then construct a short email
that invites people to join you.

Here is what the email should say:

Hi (person's name),

I have just created my business Facebook page and I've
done it with you in mind. Several times a week I will be
posting information that you can use immediately, and so
will other businesses, customers, and vendors like yourself.

I'm creating a community about (talk about your business
and your product). Please click here to get to my page
and then press the "Like" button at the top to join the
community.

I promise you will enjoy it and value from it.

Best regards,

LINKEDIN
BOOM!

The Difference Between Social Media and Business Social Media on LinkedIn.

Good news! LinkedIn is already "for business."

Go to your LinkedIn page and look at three things:

1. **How many connections do you have?**
2. **How many recommendations do you have?**
3. **What is your summary statement?**

Go look at mine. I have attracted 500+ connections – the actual number as of this date is more than 5,000 which puts me in the top 2% of the 85 million LinkedIn participants. That's a lot of connections, or should I say *a lot of possible connections.*

Those three front-page stats pretty much determine your LinkedIn prowess and prospect.

Prowess is the reputation that you have when someone else looks at your page. Prospect is your present condition and what you can hope to achieve based on what exists and what opportunities you have for growth.

LinkedIn is foundational to business social media. LinkedIn is where you should devote most of your energy during the early formation of your *Social BOOM!* process. LinkedIn requires that you have some depth as a person so that when your name is clicked on it shows some reason why someone would want to link with you.

LinkedIn is not some frivolous networking event where you can go around collecting connections like you collect business cards. It doesn't work that way.

People need to have a reason to want to connect with you. Otherwise, they will press Archive or Delete.

NOTE WELL: LinkedIn is also a place where you can broadcast your capability by joining groups and creating update messages in your profile.

EXAMPLE: I belong to a group called Sales Gravy where people post discussions. Occasionally, I will post a response in one of the discussions. I try to be provocative without being provoking, but for those of you who know me, that doesn't always work. Every time I have posted a comment on Sales Gravy, 10 people want to connect with me. Sales Gravy has approximately 7,000 members, and more than 200 are in my list of connections.

I do ask people to connect. Anytime I learn of someone, meet someone, get an email from someone, or create a new sales contact, the first thing I do is go to LinkedIn to find out more about them and ask them to join my network. And I've never used the standard line within the LinkedIn invitation. If I'm going to ask someone to join me, I personalize the message.

Go back to my LinkedIn page and take a look at some of the recommendations that people have given me. These people have said nice things about me all based on events that took place outside of LinkedIn and outside of social media.

What are you doing outside of social media that is attracting people to you inside of social media?

Social media is **ONE** brick in your foundation of success, but it is by far not the only brick. My books, my weekly article, my weekly e-zine, my speeches, and my public appearances are other bricks in my foundation.

The more bricks you have in your foundation, the more successful you will be in LinkedIn and business social media in general.

JEFFREY GITOMER

The 15 Imperatives of LinkedIn.

By Joe Soto

Let's pretend it was recently announced the world's largest networking event was open for you to attend. Let's also pretend you knew your customers and prospects would be there to talk to, share ideas with, collaborate on projects with, add value to, and be in front of. Would you go? How often would you go if this were an ongoing event with an open invitation?

ANSWER: As often as possible!

If you haven't been incorporating LinkedIn into your marketing mix, consider the latest statistics according to LinkedIn's website:

- **LinkedIn has more than 85 million members.**

- **A new member joins LinkedIn approximately every second.**

- **Executives from all Fortune 500 companies are LinkedIn members.**

I suggest you figure out linkedin before your competition does.

Are you making LinkedIn too hard? Or confusing it with something it isn't? It seems most people believe it's best used as a social networking site for posting your résumé.

The power and reach of LinkedIn far exceeds using the site just as a way to find a new career.

LinkedIn is a powerful way to:

- **Differentiate yourself and be found in a sea of competition.**

- **Generate an endless supply of leads for you and your company.**

- **Manage your online reputation and highlight your strengths.**

- **Collaborate on projects, and share files and ideas with connections.**

- **Network with like-minded professionals who will be lifelong referral partners.**

- **Make important connections that can help you close deals.**

- **Post and distribute job listings to find the best talent for your company.**

To be on the receiving end of these benefits you must do certain things deliberately and consistently each week.

There is no autopilot to LinkedIn. You can't adjust a few settings and then be on your way. LinkedIn won't do the work for you.

Here are The 15 Imperatives of LinkedIn that, if successfully acted on, will change how you market and connect with other people online:

1. Complete Your Profile. LinkedIn is very user friendly. There is no excuse for not filling out your LinkedIn profile to 100% completion.

2. Update and Engage Frequently with Your Connections. You can't expect people to pay attention to you if you never have anything to say, comment on, or contribute to. You must think of LinkedIn as an interaction tool and participate in the conversations.

3. Recommend Others. Don't just ask for recommendations. Surprise someone and give a recommendation. It will strengthen your relationship and it puts your link on someone else's profile. Oftentimes your connections will reciprocate.

4. Solve Other People's Problems. If you aren't using the LinkedIn Answers section, you are missing out on an opportunity to showcase your expertise. LinkedIn Answers will give you an open forum to solve other people's problems and ask (quality) questions to get people engaged with you.

5. Join and Participate in Groups. Get in on the conversations that are going on every day on LinkedIn, and join groups of interest to you that are relevant to you being able to add value. If people appreciate your comments, they may connect with you and eventually need your product or services.

6. Start Your Own Group. Don't just join groups; create your own group on a topic of interest for your area of expertise or on a hot topic of interest to people you want to connect with.

7. Search Companies and Harvest New Leads. Create a list of your top 50 company prospects, and then search for each company name in the "companies" section of the LinkedIn search engine. When you click on the company you are looking for, you'll notice the company profile lists all their employees (including decision makers) who also have profiles on LinkedIn. Your leads are on LinkedIn, you just have to look for them.

8. Respond to Everyone who Communicates with You.
Relationships can get started, developed, and turned into
business for you over time on LinkedIn. But you must be
timely in your responses.

9. Set Up the SlideShare Application and Add Value. Add some
visual appeal to your profile. What is your value proposition?
Put it in a PowerPoint, upload it to SlideShare (for free), and
put it on your LinkedIn profile.

10. Change Your Status Regularly. You'll be surprised by how
many people will respond to your status, much like they do
on Facebook.

11. Put a Video on Your Profile. Putting a video on your
LinkedIn profile is easy with the Google Presentation
application. A video is the best way to differentiate your
profile from others.

12. Promote Your Blog. If you have a blog (and you should),
you can put your blog feed on your LinkedIn profile, which
will update as often as you update your blog. This is another
great way to add value to others through your profile.

13. Add a Portfolio. With the Behance application you can
showcase your clients, your creative work, and additional
videos. It's free, easy to use, and supports unlimited
multimedia content.

14. Integrate Twitter. Want to increase your Twitter following?
Integrate the Tweets application into your LinkedIn profile
so your connections can be a part of the conversation on
Twitter.

15. Leverage LinkedIn's Search Power and Be Found. LinkedIn is
a search engine and has respectable authority on Google.

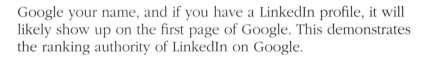

Google your name, and if you have a LinkedIn profile, it will likely show up on the first page of Google. This demonstrates the ranking authority of LinkedIn on Google.

LinkedIn's search engine within its website is where you also want to show up. Not just for your name, but also for the keywords that people are searching for people like you with. If someone types in "financial planning" the results they will see are all the profiles that have the keywords "financial planning" in them. In fact, there will be many pages and thousands of profiles that may show up in the results.

If you are a financial planner, when someone types in "financial planning," you want to have the best chance at showing up high in the search page results. Ideally, you want to show up on the first couple of pages.

Here's a simple process to rank often on the first page of search results in the "people search" on LinkedIn. (This process may not work every time, but it will work most times if done correctly.):

1. **Make the most of your headline.** Your headline is your first impression. It's what people read in the search results, and oftentimes it's the first thing they read when they go to your profile. It's also what LinkedIn's search engine will scan first for relevancy in a search. You can use up to 120 characters in your headline, so make the most of it.

2. **Make your current and past work experience keyword rich.** People may not read through your entire work history, but the search engine will find relevant keywords for what people are looking for when searching profiles. Without sounding redundant or annoying, fill out your work experience to include your keywords when you can.

LinkedIn gives you up to 1000 characters to use in your position description area, so be sure to make the most of it by weaving in relevant keywords.

3. **Make the most of the Summary section.** The Summary section is the most often missed, and yet it's the most open area for you to include keywords. LinkedIn permits you to use up to 2,000 characters in the Summary section. Use all 2,000 characters to make keyword rich statements and a keyword-rich benefit summary of how you are valuable.

4. **Specialties should equal keywords.** The Specialties section is where you should list as many keyword rich specialties (up to 500 characters) that you can think of. For example, if you are a financial planner, you might list keyword specialties such as financial planning, financial management, retirement planning, money management, and so on.

5. **Add keyword-rich website links.** In the websites editing area, instead of displaying the default "My Blog" or "My Website," click on Edit and then click on Other. This will open up an additional field for you to add a keyword phrase that describes how people can search to find your business. If you are a financial planner, you'd put the phrase "Financial Planning" in place of "My Website" and have it link to your website when they click on the keyword phrase. For your blog, you'd put "financial planning blog" as the keyword phrase.

If you're a business professional, you can't afford not to be using LinkedIn. You now have The 15 Imperatives of LinkedIn to blaze your own trail on the most popular professional social network.

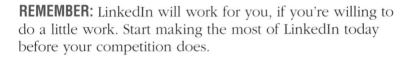

REMEMBER: LinkedIn will work for you, if you're willing to do a little work. Start making the most of LinkedIn today before your competition does.

Joe Soto is a leading expert in social media marketing with more than 10 years of experience in all aspects of sales, marketing, online lead generation, and Internet marketing.

Joe is the Founder and Chief Social Strategist of One Social Media LLC, (http://www.onesocialmedia.com) a nationally recognized social media marketing agency. His company has played a key role in the launch of social media campaigns for local, regional and national businesses and brands throughout the U.S. Clients range from a broad variety of industries.

Connect with Joe on LinkedIn at http://www.linkedin.com/in/ josephsoto.

Selling Is Social.
How to Leverage Social
Media to Make Sales.

By Noah Rickun

LinkedIn is by far the most valuable of all social media sites for salespeople. Unlike Facebook, Twitter, and YouTube, LinkedIn is all business, all the time. Interestingly, most salespeople have done little more with LinkedIn than to sign up and fill out a few résumé details. Bad move.

I have used LinkedIn to successfully prospect, appoint, connect, uncover, relate, prepare, engage, attract, qualify, close, and stay in touch with customers. At the time of this writing, I have roughly 2,500 connections. Those 2,500 "trusted friends and colleagues" (as defined by LinkedIn) connect me to 689,700 friends of friends, and almost 13,000,000 users within three degrees. The goal is to provide valuable, relevant, engaging content that your connections will want to share with *their* connections. In his *Little Black Book of Connections*, Jeffrey wrote "It's not who you know, it's who knows you." On LinkedIn, it's who knows YOU and who THEY know!

There are two ways to become known on LinkedIn – Answers[1] and Groups.[2] I suggest you spend time learning about both features and then begin to interact with others by answering questions about which you have unique or special knowledge and by joining groups that your customers and prospects belong to.

---

[1] http://learn.linkedin.com/answers/
[2] http://learn.linkedin.com/groups/

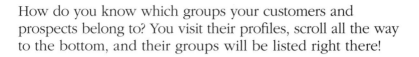
How do you know which groups your customers and prospects belong to? You visit their profiles, scroll all the way to the bottom, and their groups will be listed right there!

You can join up to 50 groups and my suggestion is you do so as soon as possible. Once you join a group, you can invite group members to connect with you in two clicks. It's the easiest method of connecting on LinkedIn, and it's a method that most people ignore.

Actually, I suggest that you join 49 groups and then create one yourself. Find a topic that you are interested in (you don't have to know anything about the topic – but you do have to be willing to dedicate a significant amount of time researching, sharing, and discussing it), search LinkedIn to ensure that somebody else hasn't already created the exact same group, and then create it.

Here's the why and the how...

Why you should create a LinkedIn Group:

1. **You become known as a person of value.** Even if you do nothing more than create the group and post interesting questions and links to articles, you are forever recognized as the group Owner.

2. **People will want to connect with you as the Owner.** I receive new invitations daily from group members who find the discussions interesting. It's an easy way to grow your network.

3. **You control the discussion.** The content is entirely up to you – meaning you can lead the discussion in a way that is interesting to you and to your prospects.

4. **You attract attention to yourself.** Every group email lists you as Owner – recipients will click on your profile.

5. **As the group Owner, you have instant communication with all members.** If you want to send a message to all of them – it only takes one click. It's the only place on LinkedIn that allows you to email blast more than 50 people at a time.

6. **Your prospects will reach out to you.** If you create the right group, lead the right discussions, and present yourself as a resource.

How to Create, Promote, Moderate, and Leverage Your Very Own LinkedIn Group:

1. **From pretty much any page on LinkedIn, select the Groups tab in the banner near the top of the page (see Figure 1).**

Figure 1

2. **Now select Create a Group (see Figure 2).**

Figure 2

3. Fill out the fields on the next page (see Figure 3). Be sure your description and summary are complete and compelling. This is how your group will be found on LinkedIn via search. You can adjust and modify most of these fields later, and you may want to experiment to see what content gets you the best results.

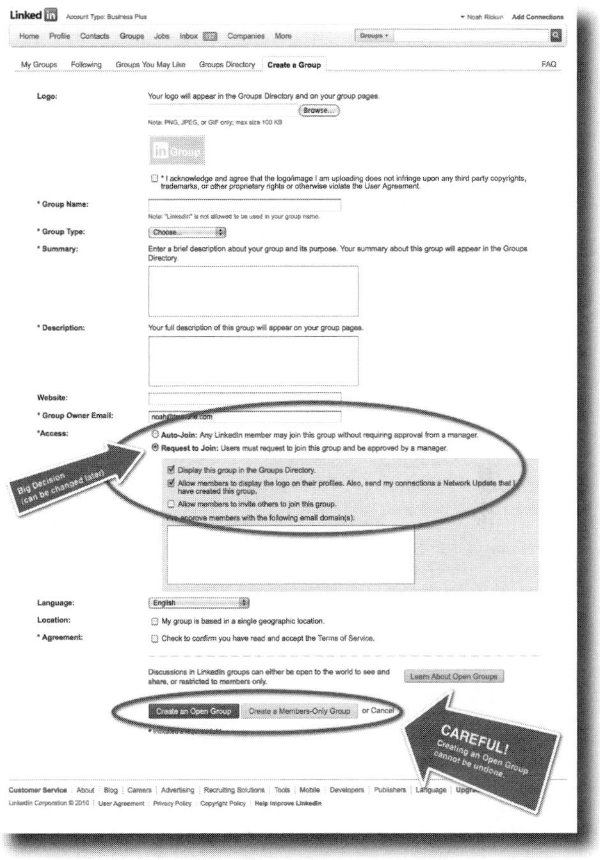

Figure 3

There are two areas, however, that you should think hard about now:

A. Access – Do you want to control membership or allow any LinkedIn member to join your group? I prefer to select Request to Join so that I can manually review each member, send a personal note welcoming him/her to the group, and ensure the requestor is not a spammer. While this is an important decision, LinkedIn does allow you to change your mind later. Try both ways to determine what works best for you.

B. Open Group versus Members-Only Group – This is LinkedIn's newest feature and your biggest decision. I've included a chart that highlights the differences of the two types of groups (see Figure 4).

Benefit	Open group *NEW*	Members-only group
Discussion visibility	Anyone*	Members only
Indexing by search engines	Yes	No
Sharing to Twitter and Facebook	Yes	No
Anyone on LinkedIn can contribute	Manager option	No

Figure 4

Depending on the content of your group's discussions – and the personality of your members – you may wish to give visibility to the entire world, or you may wish to restrict access to only those people who you grant access. Shortly after LinkedIn launched this feature, I chose to make my group *"Selling is Social – Leveraging Social Media to Make Sales"* an Open Group.

Since the discussions in my group are about social media, I figured the group should be as social as possible – which meant opening the group up to Facebook, Google, and the rest of the Web. See Figure 5 for the email I sent to my members explaining the change.

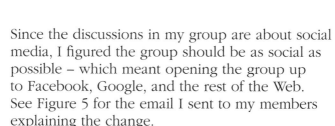

Subject: Selling is Social - Leveraging Social Media to Make Sales is now an open group

LinkedIn Groups

Group: Selling is Social - Leveraging Social Media to Make Sales
Subject: Selling is Social - Leveraging Social Media to Make Sales is now an open group

I am pleased to announce that, as the owner of this group, I have just switched us to an open discussion group. All future discussions will be fully visible, searchable, and shareable on the Web. All past discussions are now closed in a members-only archive. I look forward to our future discussions now joining the broader conversation of the wider Web, including Facebook & Google.

Good news! As you are contributing and learning from this group, you will also begin to build your personal brand and social footprint.

Contribute early, and contribute often!

At Your Service,
Noah

Posted By Noah Rickun

View or add comments »

Don't want to hear from the manager? Unsubscribe here

LinkedIn values your privacy. At no time has LinkedIn made your email address available to any other LinkedIn user without your permission. ©2010, LinkedIn Corporation.

Figure 5

4. **Invite everyone in your LinkedIn network (or a subset that you feel would be most interested in your content).** You'll simply click Manage and then Send Invitations (see Figure 6). In the Connections field you can begin typing names, or you can click the 🔲 button, which brings up your entire list of connections.

Notice you can only invite 50 connections at a time, so if you have thousands of connections on LinkedIn, you'll be clicking thousands of times.

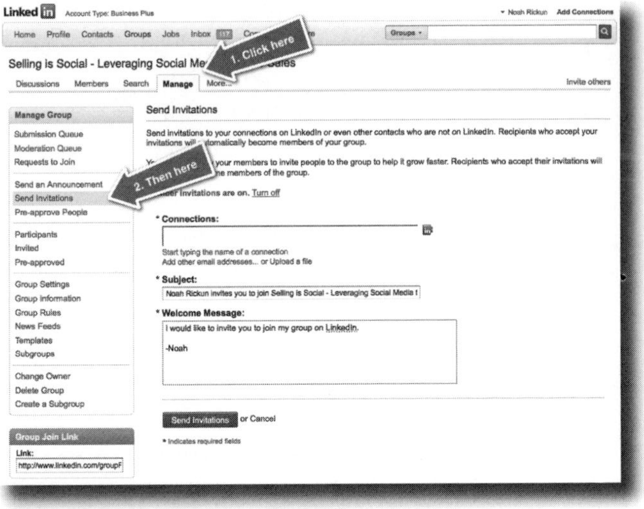

Figure 6

5. **Invite others from your email database.** Let's say you have hundreds of contacts in Outlook that you are not connected to on LinkedIn, but that you would still like to invite to your group. No problem! Export the contacts from Outlook to a .CSV file and then click Upload a File on LinkedIn just below the Connections field on the Send Invitations tab from Step 4.

6. **Make everything personal.** Owning a group allows you to demonstrate your creativity and your personal brand. One of the best ways to do this is to modify the templates LinkedIn uses for group communications. Click Templates on the Manage Group tab and you're off to the races (see Figure 7). The most important template is the Welcome Message. This is where you'll want to establish expectations and set yourself up for success. Include your contact information in the message body, and let your group members know how to connect with you.

Figure 7

7. **Discuss!** This actually has two meanings as a Group Owner. First, you'll need to start new discussions to get things started. Second, you'll want to respond and contribute to the discussions and comments.

Here are a few tips:

A. **New discussions** – Start with a welcome message and an engaging question that encourages participation. Something simple like, "Welcome to the XYZ Group! Please introduce yourself below and let everyone know what your experience with XYZ has been." The more you involve your members immediately, the more they will be involved in the future.

B. **Your responses** – Owning a group can be a lonely adventure, so when you do receive a comment, or when group members start their own discussions, be sure to respond!

Begin your response with a sincere appreciation and then help move the discussion forward. Sometimes you'll be answering a question, sometimes you'll point the member to a help forum, and sometimes you'll simply say "Right on!" Whatever you do, though, don't be silent. You've created a group, you've asked people to join, and you've asked them to contribute. When they actually do post, reward them with your time and your feedback. This alone will do wonders to make your group successful.

8. **Moderate.** Yes, it's possible that one of your members will post something irrelevant or offensive. Yes, it's possible that one of your members will only be interested in shameless self-promotion. Yes, it's possible that one of your members will violate the group rules you've created. So, can you simply delete the comment or in extreme cases, kick the member out? Yes, it's possible! You can delete any comment you'd like, you can flag comments as inappropriate, you can block a member from contributing, and you can even go as far as deleting a member from your group altogether. Since creating my group, I have yet to use any of these moderation features. LinkedIn is a very professional forum, and I find that most users are professional in their activities, but it's good to know that LinkedIn itself has given Group Owners the tools if needed. Just don't abuse your police powers – your members will be less likely to contribute if you delete opposing viewpoints rather than discuss them!

9. **Leverage.** Hey, you own a group! Put it on your business card, in your email signature, and on your website. If your group gets good enough, you can even call hard-to-reach people and ask them to contribute content for your members' consumption. After all, it sure beats cold calling!

Follow the preceding steps, and you'll be well on your way to owning and mastering your group. If you'd like to learn more, feel free to join my group, "Selling Is Social," to see what I'm doing.

ONE FINAL NOTE: LinkedIn changes features often and it's important you stay up to date. Here's the best place to keep an eye on what's new: http://blog.linkedin.com/category/new-linkedin-features/

Stay Connected!

Noah Rickun is a leader, thinker, and speaker. Before becoming the CEO of Jeffrey Gitomer's TrainOne (a world leader in online, interactive sales training and personal development), he built a $20 million division within a major automotive remanufacturer while earning his law degree from Marquette University at night.

As a Gitomer-Certified Speaker, Noah now delivers customized and personalized seminars on sales, customer loyalty, and personal development to companies worldwide.

For more information about Noah, visit http://www.Rickun.com.

LinkedIn for Anyone
and Everyone.

By The LinkedIn Rockstars, Mike O'Neil and Lori Ruff

One does not get to a polished image without polishing.

And just like the band that does not start out with the right sound, consistent practice over time is what gets them the perfect sound, the perfect image, the perfect brand. The path that winds through the world of social media is not something one can walk down quickly, nor will the experiences of others make it completely successful for you.

Rather, even when working with a seasoned professional, it is that priceless time in the trenches, pushing the limits, getting things wrong, and getting them right that makes the finished consult and product so useful, so perfect for you.

Management has valid concerns about the use of social media at the office. Reports of Facebook and Twitter abuse are only the tip of the iceberg. Companies seem to have a different view of LinkedIn however. It is widely recognized as a business tool akin to Hoovers, Harte-Hanks, Jigsaw, and others.

LinkedIn comes down to two powerful elements – a database engine and an integrated communications engine. Let us illustrate. LinkedIn users are simply records in the LinkedIn database: so are employers, educational institutions, others. We are all just data records, and in some cases interconnected data records. This simply mirrors real life, doesn't it? People have relationships with one another (but not everyone) as well as with companies, employers, interest groups, and the like.

The Integrated Alliances LinkedIn Business Methodology

Step 1: The LinkedIn Profile. Before you do anything else, it is imperative to get your LinkedIn profile spiffin' for business. Look worthy of the business you seek to find from others.

Moving to Step 2 generates traffic to your profile: traffic that can be attracted or repelled by what they see. It is up to you; you don't get credit for professional accomplishments that you don't tell readers of your profile about.

Step 2: Build your LinkedIn Network. Sly and the Family Stone said it best, "Different strokes for different folks." The type of network that makes the most sense for you depends on your role and why you are on LinkedIn in the first place. Here are some examples:

Job seeker/Career development. Aside from the obvious (recruiters, HR professionals, hiring managers) you also need to connect to people in your industry (peers) and in the companies you want to work for.

Seeking business opportunities (i.e., sales, business development). You may need a large network as well, but you absolutely need a targeted network. Spend extra time on specific subsets of the population who you do business with as well as those who typically refer business to you. Look at your current customers. What data is in their profiles? Using this information to add more people who look like your current (or best) customers and partners will naturally increase your ability to find more good business.

Marketing. Marketing is about attracting NEW people to engage your organization in business. A large network has infinitely larger marketing potential, as large as possible some might say. As one's network gets larger, more decision makers enter it. Sounds simple, right?

Executives. Yes, executives need to be on LinkedIn as well. People who consider doing business with your company will look to see who is leading the band. Do the CEO and his team have rockin' LinkedIn profiles? If not, it can hurt the company image. Your network should be filled with peers and people in direct report roles, too.

Step 3: Searching. Now that you've completed your profile and have an appropriate network for your job role, you can begin to search for what you need and get real results. LinkedIn's advanced search function delivers amazing results. These can be further filtered and refined to find the most qualified candidates, leads, prospects, or partners possible.

Step 4: Engage. Once you find who you are looking for, consider the best method to reach out and engage them in a business conversation. The LinkedIn options include Invitations, Introductions, Messages, InMails, Emails, and the old fashion analog means – phone, postal mail, and "just dropping by." Most of the online options have limits.

SPECIAL NOTE ON INVITATIONS: Personalize your invitation with information gleaned from the LinkedIn profile, especially the Interests and Groups sections near the bottom. Be concise. LinkedIn provides just 300 characters and no links or email addresses allowed in your invitation. A nice signature line to create a brand impression will help. Here is a good example of an invitation:

> *Bob:*
>
> *I see you work at Verizon. I'm a former telecom pro. I've got great contacts to share with you. Could we connect on LinkedIn?*
>
> *Mike O'Neil*
> *Speaker/Trainer/Writer*
> *Integrated Alliances*

Step 5: Do Business! Work to engage others appropriately. Your first communications with another on LinkedIn should not be a hard sales push. (Talk about a turn-off!) Consider LinkedIn to be the Chamber of Commerce of online social networks. It is for business professionals to network and engage. Act appropriately. If you have questions, contact The LinkedIn Rockstars. Our team is here to help.

The LinkedIn Rockstars, Mike O'Neil and Lori Ruff, lead Integrated Alliances, the nation's foremost LinkedIn and social media training firm.

Highly sought-after speakers, both individually and together, Mike and Lori address executives, sales teams, recruiters, and other professional teams in private business sessions and at corporate and association conferences and conventions.

To connect with Mike and Lori, call (866) 516-7823 or visit them online at http://www.RockstarNetworking.com.

TWITTER BOOM!

The Difference Between Social Media and Business Social Media on Twitter.

Take a look at your Twitter page.

Oh wait, maybe you don't have one. That's because you think tweeting is somewhere between "I'm taking a shower," to a waste of your time.

The fact is you don't know what to tweet, you don't know when to tweet, and you don't know how to tweet.

CONFESSION ONE: I am not a world-class Twitter expert, but I do have more than 25,000 Twitter followers, which puts me in the top 5% of the 175 million that do tweet. So I must know something.

CONFESSION TWO: Before I started I thought Twitter was a stupid waste of time. I was wrong.

CONFESSION THREE: I have a platform and a large base of followers from my other books, seminars, and promotions. And especially from my weekly email magazine which provided me the basis of attraction.

Throughout the course of all Twitter explanations in this book, you will find the words retweet or retweetable. They are 50% of the basis of success in Twitter. The other 50% is someone clicking on the link that you provide and taking some kind of action. But the basis of success in Twitter for business is value messaging, or to keep a common language, value tweeting.

A value tweet is a tweet that people would find so interesting or so valuable that they are compelled to retweet that message to others.

JEFFREY GITOMER

I Tweet, Therefore I Am.
Who Am You?

I resisted as long as I could – partially because my understanding of it was somewhere around zero, and partly – okay mostly, because I thought it was going to be a waste of my time.

I was wrong. Way wrong. Way, way wrong.

After a brief, but intensive education from my friend Jeff Jarvis (author of *What Would Google Do?*) and continued prodding by Rick Johnson (CEO of Kadro Solutions), I completely changed my opinion. And made a plan of action.

I registered. I obtained my name (Gitomer). And I tweeted three times in the first 24 hours.

At the end of the first day, I had more than 300 followers. At the end of the first month, I had almost 5,000 followers. My goal is to have 100,000 followers.

And I'm doing it without gimmicks, spam, or reporting news (other than mine). I have a Twitter strategy and philosophy.

Everything I do has a link to my Twitter page, especially my email magazine and the front page of my website. I've also added a live Twitter feed to my blog. I intend to use Twitter to provide readers and followers with thoughts, help, answers, and information that is useful and retweetable to their followers.

Here are a few examples of my tweets so far:

- The strongest salesman on your team is a testimonial from a loyal customer. Testimonials are proof. Gitomer

- It costs no extra money to be friendly. How friendly are you? Gitomer

- The importance of asking the right questions lies somewhere between sale and no sale. What are you asking? Gitomer

- There's no prize for second place in sales. It's gold, or go home. Gitomer

- The two BEST places for a sales appointment: Breakfast and lunch. Relaxed atmosphere and no interruptions. Gitomer

- You will succeed far greater at something you love to do. What do you really love? Is that what you're doing? Gitomer

- Don't set goals, set intentions. Whatever you intend to do will happen. Without intention, goals go unachieved. Gitomer

- If you are consistently blaming other people, guess what Bubba – it ain't them. Gitomer

- If you believe in your company, if you believe in your product, if you believe in yourself – you will march to success. Gitomer

- Failure is not about insecurity, or bad luck. It's about lack of proper execution. Gitomer

- You control the most important tool in selling, your mind. Gitomer

On Mother's Day I tweeted: *"If you have nothing nice to say about someone, say nothing." Said by your mother. Honor her today, She was right. Gitomer*

Notice my name is at the end of each tweet. That's because those quotes are mine. I wrote them. I don't quote other people. I quote myself. When I get retweeted I build my own brand and awareness and gain new followers.

Here are a few of my plans and ideas for the subject matter of my future tweets – feel free to use them or alter the strategy to suit your situation:

- **Post a daily sales tip.**

- **Give information as to my travels and where people can register for my public events and see my live seminars.**

- **Post information regarding new ideas.**

- **Post personal recommendations of every sort – from restaurants to books, from people to places, from shops to hotels. Maybe even airlines. Maybe.**

- **Ask for information and help when I travel to a new city.**

- **Create local gatherings.**

What is Twitter to me? It's an opportunity to deliver short personal messages to business connections and friends to let them know what I'm thinking and what I'm doing.

Understanding Twitter and the Power of "Retweet."

I asked an audience of 200 mature salespeople and sales managers, "How many of you have a Twitter account with more than 500 followers?"

Two people raised their hand.
One of them was me.

I couldn't believe it, so I asked again. Same response. Yikes.

It seems as though the mature (seasoned) salespeople are resisting Twitter or simply do not understand the power in it and efficacy of it.

With an estimated 175 million accounts and millions of tweets a day, there MAY just be something to it. Especially because the Fortune 1000s are tweeting. Every newspaper and news agency is tweeting. Thousands of small businesses are tweeting.

What are you doing?

Are you tweeting every day?

Or are you stymied by the process and don't quite know what to do? (Like most people.)

WARNING: Twitter for business has nothing to do with being in your pajamas, having a tough day, heading to the office, or other inane useless information. It also has nothing to do with "tweeple," "tweeps," or other buzzwords that are cute and condescending.

- **Twitter is about informing.**
- **Twitter is about passing on information.**
- **Twitter is about value messages.**
- **Twitter is about connecting.**

Twitter is about others finding value in your messages or information and passing it on to others. And when you're retweeted, it's proof that your message had enough value, content, or vital information that people in your network were willing to pass it on to their network. Cool.

BONUS: Your message, your tweet, is actually exposed to 175 million users through Twitter's storing and searching features.

The key action to become searchable is the hashtag. If you want to attract others who may be also tagging or searching for the categories that you're tweeting about, using the hashtag will group your tweets with others of a like nature.

My subjects are sales, loyalty, trust, attitude, buying motives, presentation skills, networking, and success.

Yours might be cooking, golden retrievers, swimming, Phillies, Yankees, travel, cats, or whatever interests you. People tweet about everything under the sun, and you can find them globally in a millisecond.

You can also aggregate your tweets to appear on your LinkedIn account and on your business Facebook page.

In short, you can send information to your entire network every day. And if others find it interesting, or valuable, they will send it to their network.

How does a daily value tweet help you?

1. **It challenges you to think and write.** Daily discipline.

2. **It challenges you to create viral messages so that you become better known as a person of value.**

3. **It challenges you to create the REAL law of attraction.** Attraction = potential customer.

3.5 **People will proactively connect with you.** If they agree with you, and they respect you, they'll tell others to connect with you as well.

You can also create category lists of any kind to compile your own "best of" by subject. Others wanting information on the same subject will find you. People add me to their list under categories like business success, personal inspiration, and sales. So far, I have been added to 1,187 lists that are reposting my tweets. You can make your own lists, but the key is to be added to other's lists.

By choice, I do not use Twitter for interactive communication.

Occasionally I'll ask a question of my followers (and get instant response), or tell them of an upcoming public seminar, but for the most part I tweet thought-provoking statements. Retweetable statements.

Yesterday I tweeted: *It's easy to find and attract great people – just be a great person who does great things. #Gitomer.* It got a hundred retweets in 24 hours and many comments on my LinkedIn account.

Today I'm tweeting: *An objection is actually a sales barrier. Lower the barrier, and reduce their perceived risk, and the sale is yours. #Gitomer*

There is a secret to Twitter success. And it's the same secret for all of social media, especially business social media: Wake up and WRITE.

JEFFREY GITOMER

Sandy Carter Leads (Socially) from the Front Row.

An hour before my IBM leadership and sales seminar was about to begin, I walked the audience.

Some people came up to greet me and shake my hand, recognizing me or my trademarked maintenance shirt – while others (most of them) glanced at me, assumed I was a maintenance guy, and went about their business as though I was invisible.

The front row of the room was empty save for one person.

"Hi, my name is Jeffrey Gitomer. Are you by chance Sandy Carter?" "Yes, I am," she smiled.

We exchanged pleasantries and talked a bit about the event and how excited and honored I was to be presenting.

Sandy Carter, for the uninformed, is an iconic IBM employee. Although her official title is Vice President of Software Business Partners & Midmarket, she is unofficially the Queen of Business Social Media. She has been a hands-on, guiding leader inside Big Blue for the past 20 years.

By no coincidence, Sandy selected the front row at my seminar. She tweeted the entire time. And not one person had the confidence or the guts to sit beside her.

I began my talk with a challenge to the audience about their social media presence, and their understanding of the opportunity that social media presents.

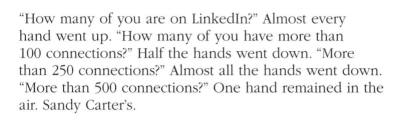

"How many of you are on LinkedIn?" Almost every hand went up. "How many of you have more than 100 connections?" Half the hands went down. "More than 250 connections?" Almost all the hands went down. "More than 500 connections?" One hand remained in the air. Sandy Carter's.

"How many of you have a Twitter account that you actually use?" A (very) few hands went up. "How many of you have more than 500 Twitter followers?" Three hands. "One thousand followers?" One hand remained in the air. Sandy Carter's. "Five thousand followers?" Carter's hand stayed up. "TEN thousand followers?" Carter's hand stayed up, as the audience gasped.

She's a 20-year, loyal IBM employee. She's responsible for the success of more than 1,700 people. She blogs to thousands, tweets to 21,000, and has a LinkedIn connection factor of more than 1,000. She has won 14 marketing innovation awards. And she lives at or near the edge. She is the classic dictionary definition of "leading by example."

Sandy has written two books (while most leaders are still thinking about theirs). *The New Language of Business: SOA and Web 2. 0* and *The New Language of Marketing 2.0.* She'll have her third book written and launched before 99.9% of all other leaders on the planet (with the same amount of tenure) have their first chapter written.

How's your book coming along?

I am presenting Sandy as an example of an executive using business social media because she is IN the fire every day.

My interview with Sandy was electric. You could feel her strength of character and determination on the phone. Here are a few examples of on the edge:

RESULTS FROM TAKING A RISK: "When I tweeted, 'Analytics is the new black,' I was hoping it would get a lot more retweets than it did. I did receive a lot of comments on my blog and four or five customers have asked for me to come do briefings with them because they want to understand what social analytics is and what it can do for their company."

TAKING A RISK TO BE FIRST AND WINNING: "When we first started looking at social media, IBM was getting into what I would consider some very cool technology areas. I decided that communicating through social media channels could make us a true technology leader, so I took the plunge. It's working better than I hoped."

LEARNING TO MASTER BEFORE DELEGATING: "I first started leveraging social media personally. I found out how it was allowing me to make connections and have a dialog. As soon as we started the new portfolio as the solution, I instantly added social media into what we were doing to really get the buzz and the energy up. The first thing I did was begin with a blog and then posted a really cool YouTube video."

LEADERSHIP CHALLENGE: "Social media is remarkable. What can happen on Twitter or on a blog can go either good or bad. And as a leader you're very vulnerable. You literally have to be pristine in what you are talking about because someone will take it the wrong way."

LEADERSHIP ACTION: "I want to be an evangelist to my customers and partners. We just did a survey of 3,000 of my partners and we found that 34% are already using social media as a sales tool.

The other 66% said 'I haven't started' or 'I have started but I really don't know what I'm doing and I need some education or training.' So we started a series of online training classes and I've done a personal lunch and learn series. Throughout IBM and with my partner community, I can have 3,000 people on a lunch and learn where we go through how to use Twitter, how to create a blog, or how to create links onto Flickr and YouTube. It's pretty amazing how many people are trying to learn. If you don't do it yourself, then you can't teach it."

MAKING A DIFFERENCE: Sandy started a super women's group at IBM that is now about 15,000 to 16,000 women strong. "What we do is focus on skills like networking, technology, social media, getting together and forming the community, and how to make IBM an even better company and better place for women."

Sandy Carter is a true leader. I have attempted to honor her strategies and achievements, but it would take more than these few pages.

I am challenging you, the reader, to study these online accomplishments, and compare them to yours over a 20-year period. After you read her books, follow her on Twitter, and subscribe to her blog, you'll have a better idea of her depth, and the online example she is setting globally.

Free GitXBit... If you're interested in learning more about Sandy Carter, go to http://www.gitomer.com, and enter the word SANDY in the GitBit box.

Welcome to the
Ultimate Cocktail Party

By Sally Hogshead

You walk through the door to the party... and WOW. It's loud. And chaotic. And confusing. And buzzing with an incomprehensible frenzy of people talking all at once.

But then, after a moment, you spot your buddy nearby. He introduces you into his circle. Turns out, his friends all work in your same field. Cool.

Nearby, you begin to recognize people you've been wanting to meet: a potential new vendor, a white-hot leader in your industry, and is that your CEO in the corner?

And wait – look! Over there – it's your biggest competitor, chatting with a big circle. You sidle over, nonchalantly listening in as she reveals a few key details about her upcoming product launch.

Your eyes continue scanning the party, and suddenly, you spy a flock of potential customers, chatting informally. Jackpot! They're perfectly positioned for you to effortlessly join in. Hello, sale.

By this point in the party you're confident and at ease, and having a pretty terrific time. What initially looked like a giant networking clustermess now feels familiar, filled with mingling clusters of diverse groups. All around you, each group engages in spirited conversations and friendly banter, with professional introductions and shared interests, questions and answers, ideas and opinions, and above all, connections.

This, my friends is Twitter: The ultimate cocktail party. Here, you won't find platters of chicken nuggets. But you will find juicy nuggets of insight, along with introductions, referrals, and best of all, plenty opportunities to sell.

As with any great party, Twitter allows different people, even with totally different points of view, to express themselves and share ideas. You quickly figure out who you want to hang out with: *the people who add value.*

How can you add value to your Twitter conversations? *Earlier in this book, I described all kinds of ways you can immediately create fascinating messages. Once you start to develop more charismatic and persuasive content, here's what will help you build your own Twitter party network:*

1. You don't have to be flashy or fabulous, but you do have to **be smart and bring something new to the discussion.**

2. Know **when to talk** and **when to listen**.

3. **Let your personality shine through.** If you have a serious way of communicating, great. But don't take yourself so-o-o seriously that you turn into a soulless typist.

4. **Don't pick a fight** unless controversy is consistent with your core message. It's okay to be provocative, and even contrarian, but remember that it's still a public forum filled with inherently social people.

5. **Ask smart questions** that contribute to the conversation. Or better yet, ask questions that will start conversations.

6. **Develop original thoughts and observations.** Don't just copy and repeat. Draw upon your unique experiences and history, then share it with others.

7. **Listen** to other guests, especially those you'd like to woo into conversation with you, before you jump into a direct conversation with them.

So, who does NOT add value to a party?

- **The over-eager sales professional** who only talks about himself. He shoves a business card in your hand, relentlessly pushing his own agenda. On Twitter, this person will tweet endlessly about himself and his products, hammering the exact same points, without ever contributing relevant ideas or insight.

- **The bore** who does talk (and talk and talk), but doesn't say anything relevant. On Twitter, this bore constantly tweets about things like the weather, or what her cat ate for lunch. Or worse, sends an endless stream of quotes from famous dead people. Yawn!

- **The wallflower** who never says anything worth noticing. He lurks around the perimeter of the room, not joining the conversation. On Twitter, you don't have to unnaturally inflate your personality, but you'll meet the by infusing your conversation with your own natural point of view and style.

- **The jerk.** Ugh. This obnoxious guest is always interrupting others. Always trotting out an unsolicited, critical opinion, tossing firebombs into the conversation.

What's your goal at the party? Twitter is free, however, there's opportunity cost involved: the time you spend reading and writing tweets is time you can't spend on other marketing efforts. Like all social media, it requires a commitment of time and energy.

To justify this effort, build your Twitter empire around clear goals. Here are some examples:

- **Build your network, and sphere of influence:** Spread your ideas to an ever-increasing circle of followers who rely on you for insight.

- **Reach potential customers:** Say you're a travel agent. You tweet about little-known reasons to vacation in Dominican Republic. If I'm planning a sunny vacation, well, you just won yourself a new customer.

- **Do reconnaissance on competitors.** Follow the companies you're competing against – and the individual leaders within those companies. Watch how they're interacting with customers, and what clues they share about developments. (The same applies for companies that you'd like to be hired by. Follow your favorite companies, and the people within them. You can often glean savvy insider hints about goings-on and its internal culture).

- **Learn what customers and partners are saying about your company and products:** Worried you'll see people complaining? Yes, maybe you will. Those conversations are already taking place, and you can't control them. But you can respond. And you can participate in learning. Get contact info and reach out. If those situations are occurring, you want to be there.

- **Learn more about niche areas of professional interest:** In an application such as TweetDeck, set up searches for specific industry terms related to your main interest.

- **Introduce yourself to potential partners or employers:** If you're eager for an introduction to a prominent industry leader, find out if he or she has a Twitter account, then observe what and how the person tweets.

Use the "@Reply" feature to comment on her tweets, or retweet ("RT") her to spread her Twitter glory to your network. Once you're on her radar, you can tweet her a question or useful piece of info yourself. Many high-level leaders are more likely to respond to a message on Twitter than in their spam-drenched email inbox.

Yes, it takes some work. But rather than paying for marketing results, you're actively earning them.

Why you need to join in the Twitter party. Five years ago, if you wanted to market yourself or your products, you needed cash. Lots. If someone at the big ad agencies had raised her hand and announced, "Hey, pretty soon companies will be able to market themselves very effectively and inexpensively by 'tweeting' 140 character messages of value on Twitter" … well… (stifled chuckle) let's just say, that person wouldn't have been taken very seriously.

In the modern playing field, success and failure is no longer based on having the biggest budget. The winners are the ones with the most compelling, meaningful, and valuable points. If you don't have a bigger budget than your competitors, no problem – as long as you find ways to connect with the consumer.

People and companies can no longer buy influence – now they must earn it. And nowhere is there a better place to earn influence than the cocktail party of Twitter.

Consider this your personal invitation to the party. And when you arrive, come find me on the dancefloor: @sallyhogshead.

Cheers!

You don't need 10,000 tweets to get 20,000 followers. You need 200 quality, relevant, valuable messages that are retweetable.

JEFFREY GITOMER

Three Things Businesses Totally Miss About Twitter.

By Mark Schaefer

Twitter is one of the most important business development tools ever created.

Does that surprise you? Have you thought of Twitter as some kiddie toy or another social media network for Justin Bieber fans? It's time to reconsider!

I've taught hundreds of business professionals through my social media marketing classes and have found three common obstacles to understanding – and leveraging – Twitter as an effective business development channel.

1. Misunderstanding the channel. Twitter isn't about B2B sales or B2C sales. It's about P2P networking. Person to person.

If you're in a business that can benefit from networking at an industry event or a chamber of commerce meeting, then Twitter is perfect for you. But like any networking, it's about building long-term relationships, not making a quick sale.

Connections lead to recognition. Recognition leads to awareness. Awareness leads to friendships. And friendships lead to business relationships built on trust.

THE MOST COMMON MISTAKE: Businesses think of Twitter as a personal broadcasting network instead of a relationship-building opportunity. Too many people simply are trying to fit old media advertising messages into the new media – with disastrous results.

People are sick of being sold to. They are sick of being marketed to. They come to social networks for fun, information, connection, and entertainment.

Keep this in mind as you develop your social media presence. And remember that your presence starts with your online image.

What image are you presenting on your Twitter account? Your company logo? Is it a building? Your product? How does that enable personal connection? It's not easy for people to relate to a photograph of a building or a truck.

What are you tweeting about? Your new EPA designation? An industry award? A quarterly sales record? Sure, some of that is important. But if you met somebody and that is ALL they talked about you would look for the nearest exit?

BE A PERSON: Be real, be human, and be authentically helpful. Then you'll genuinely attract attract people who are interested in you and your business.

2. Misunderstanding the payoff. There are many businesses that are starry-eyed over the social media hype and expect quick results and sales. And while that certainly can happen, you're missing out if you don't consider the broad spectrum of potential business benefits, even if you never make a direct sale!

It's a shame that companies quickly dismiss social media marketing because they can't calculate a measurable ROI. Don't get me wrong. For many well-managed companies, this mindset has worked well in the past.

But to really understand the opportunities of Twitter, you need to consider the wide range of potential benefits:

- **Competitive intelligence**
- **Market insight**
- **A new supplier or business partner**
- **Publicity**
- **Brand awareness**
- **An idea**
- **New products**
- **Customer service**
- **Education**
- **Quick solutions to problems**
- **And yes, even lead generation**

These benefits are being realized by many businesses every day, yet most of these would be very hard to display in an Excel spreadsheet or incorporate into an ROI calculation. So stop trying to do it!

I once recognized somebody at a networking meeting from his Twitter picture. Because I had been following his "tweets," I knew he just started an online business, he has two little boys, he recently vacationed in California, and he is a baseball fanatic.

I had never met him before, but when I introduced myself, he gave me a bear hug and greeted me like a long-lost friend! Through my stream of information on Twitter, he felt like he knew me, too. We had formed an instant connection that led to friendship and trust.

The meeting was about to start and we didn't have time to chat, but we exchanged phone numbers and committed to meet for coffee the following week to talk about ways we could work together.

He eventually became one of my best customers.

Now, how many cold calls would you have to make to find a new business connection who greets you with a hug on the first meeting? I had effectively used Twitter to prepopulate the business relationship! And yes, it did eventually result in sales, but more important, it resulted in a new business connection that could result in opportunities for years to come.

I still observe many companies stumbling around trying to calculate their return on investment while their competitors are establishing a social media foothold on this powerful business communication and networking platform.

To really succeed, businesses have to adopt a new, long-term, relationship-oriented mindset about the business benefits.

3. Misunderstanding the strategy. Business is all about speed. And whatever you did yesterday is not good enough or fast enough for today. It is very tempting to try to take shortcuts to find ways to reach people on Twitter and develop business benefits as rapidly as possible. But it can't be done. Just like building any long-term friendship, there simply is no shortcut to developing an effective, targeted Twitter tribe.

I recently received this tweet: "Thanks for the follow. I'm gaining daily new targeted followers with http://www.wyz.com. It's the company everyone uses. Let me know."

While that might sound like a great idea, it's a scam. Unfortunately where corruption can occur, corruption WILL occur and Twitter is no different. There is a cottage industry dedicated to building accounts of blank followers and then selling them for instant "credibility" to unsuspecting buyers.

A friend recently called to tell me he had just bought a Twitter account and had inherited 6,000 followers. "Now, what do I do next?" he asked. My reply: "Start over."

There are plenty of scams out there. Avoid them all.

Instead, here is a three-stage strategy common to every Twitter to success story (which I explain in depth in my book, The Tao of Twitter*):*

Targeted connections. No amount of work, time, or dedication to marketing and social media networking will work if you haven't surrounded yourself with people who might be interested in you and what you have to say. While the story I told about meeting my new friend at the networking meeting might have seemed like luck, it wasn't. The conditions were ripe for this connection because both of us had systematically surrounded ourselves with people likely to want to know us, learn from us, and help us.

Think about Twitter followers like atoms flying around inside a chemist's test tube, bumping into each other randomly. Obviously the more atoms you have in the tube, the better your chances that a reaction will occur!

But every chemical reaction needs a catalyst, and on Twitter that catalyst is *meaningful content.* Content is the currency of the social web, and sharing that content is the catalyst to new relationships and business benefits.

Content can come in many forms. For example, it might be:

- **A link to your blog or other blogs relevant to your target audience**
- **A retweeted message from others**
- **A link to comments you create on LinkedIn and other platforms**
- **An anecdote from your day**
- **An opinion about a special event, something in the news, a development in your company or community**
- **Interesting online content from your business, or a white paper, e-book, or industry report**

Content is the value that attracts and retains targeted followers to your Twitter account. You need to commit and be present in the Twitter community at least several times a week.

And finally, none of this success can happen without:

Authentic Helpfulness. This third and final factor is the one that is the most misused and the most misunderstood, and simply ignored by folks using Twitter today. This is an extremely important and subtle difference between traditional sales/marketing and new media.

At least for the foreseeable future, there will be a place for cold calling and the traditional sales function. When you schedule a call with a new client in many industries, they expect you to go through a tailored and well-rehearsed sales pitch.

But that simply doesn't work on the social web. In an always on, real-time, global world of business communications, the priority is on human interaction and trust established by kindness and helpfulness, not sales charts.

I hope this provides an introduction that sparks enough interest for you to explore the possibility of driving business benefits through Twitter.

Remember that neither a book nor a class can teach you how to have an effective online presence. You need to immerse yourself in the channel and the experiment – and maybe even have some fun along the way!

Mark W. Schaefer is a nationally recognized blogger, educator, business consultant and author of The Tao of Twitter.

Mark has worked in global sales, PR, and marketing positions for nearly 30 years and now provides consulting services as Executive Director of Schaefer Marketing Solutions. He is an adjunct marketing professor at Rutgers University's MBA program and has advanced degrees in marketing and organizational development. Mark holds seven patents and is author of the blog {grow}, one of the Ad Age "Power 150" marketing blogs of the world.

For more info, visit http://www.businessesGROW.com.

The 12 Things I Have Learned About Twitter.

By Chris Hamilton

I have been using Twitter for less than a year. I didn't understand the point of Twitter at first, but now I understand its power and importance.

I use Twitter every day to promote my daily blog posts and other events or items that I think people may find interesting.

As with anything you do, always learning new and innovative ways to use the service is key.

Here are The 12 Things I Have Learned About Twitter:

1. You have to be on Twitter on a regular basis. If you are going to use Twitter, make sure that you are using it every day or every couple of days. You have to basically make a commitment to yourself to make sure that you will use Twitter every day (or every other day) in order to see the results of your efforts.

2. Twitter can be a great source of traffic to your website or blog. I use Twitter three to four times a day to promote my daily blog posts. According to my traffic report, Twitter is my third best source of traffic to my site behind Google and direct traffic. Typically it represents between 12% and 15% of all traffic to my site.

3. Twitter is a great way to share information about stuff you want to share. I use Twitter to inform people about my newsletter, any webinars that I have going on, and any events that I am putting on.

4. You have to respond to people who contact you. If people reach out to you on Twitter, make sure that you respond to them. There are a couple of ways that people can contact you. The first way is using the @ symbol with your user name and the other way is through a DM (Direct Message). Also, if someone retweets one of your messages, make sure that you show them that you appreciate it and send them a thank-you message to acknowledge the retweet.

5. You have to get your message across in as few words as possible. Since you have only 140 characters to get your point across, you really have to think about the message that you want to produce. Make sure that your message is hard hitting and to the point.

6. Leave at least 20 characters left in your post so it can be retweeted without shortening your message. One cool thing about Twitter is that it is full of like-minded people who may want to share your message with their followers. In this case, they can retweet your message. Basically, they take the message that you wrote and share it with their followers. In order to make sure that your original message is intact, leave at least 20 characters so that the message can be retweeted. The reason for this is that the beginning of a retweet starts with "RT @username" and is usually about 20 characters long. If your message is too long to be retweeted, then it probably won't be retweeted.

7. Use hashtags to be found easier. Hashtags are what people use to categorize their Tweets by subject. Go to the search box on Twitter and type in #(your subject of interest).

8. Tweets have a very short lifespan. Because there are a lot of people tweeting all the time, your message becomes one in millions per day. If you feel that you aren't being heard, don't worry, people will hear you, just write some thought provoking or catchy tweets and they will come.

9. It's a great way to find information or look for opportunities. I use Twitter to find opportunities for work or to find information that I might find interesting. The search box in Twitter is a great way to find information. For example, let's say you are looking for a sales role in your area, you could type in "job, sales, your city" and see the results. It's amazing how much information people put on Twitter.

10. Use Hootesuite or some sort of service to schedule your Tweets. Since I work all day, I can't be on Twitter all the time. The solution for this is to use a service like Hootesuite to schedule your tweets. These services allow you to schedule your tweets at different times and on any day that you want.

11. If you want your message to be heard, I find the best time to Tweet is between 9 AM and 3 PM Eastern Standard Time.

12. My Twitter followers are great. I have met a lot of great people on Twitter. My followers engage me in conversations, ask me questions, tell me stuff that's going on in their world, help me out when I need it, and give me support. Even though I have over 12,000 followers between two Twitter accounts, I appreciate every single one of them.

Here is how I promote my daily blog posts on Twitter:

1. Write three to four overviews that are up to 120 characters long. Each overview has to have enough info to make someone want to click on the link. I use a Word document to write my thoughts down, and then I make sure that they are going to fit within the 140 character limit.

2. Use a URL shortener to reduce the URL or website address size. Twitter has a limit of 140 characters. You need as many characters as possible to get your point across. If you have a web address that is 110 characters long, then you have only 30 characters to get your point across. A URL shortener will take a long URL and shorten it to 20 characters or so – and you can customize it. (Bit.ly is the service that I use, but if you want to find one that fits for what you need, search online for "url shortener.") Copy the URL (web address) for your blog post from the address bar of your web browser and paste it into the shortener box in bit.ly. Click shorten and you will receive a new URL. A great benefit that bit.ly has is instant analytics. You can see such information as; how many people have clicked on your link, where it came from, how many retweets there have been, and more.

3. Rinse and repeat every time you have new content that you want to share with the world.

Chris Hamilton has had a 25-year career in sales and marketing with different companies ranging from startups to some of the top Fortune 500 companies.

Chris writes a daily blog, Sales Tip A Day, found at http://www.SalesTipADay.com, which helps salespeople, entrepreneurs, and small and medium-sized businesses with sales and marketing tips.

Chris also runs a sales and marketing consultancy firm that helps individuals and companies achieve sales and marketing success through proven online and real-world processes.

Follow Chris on Twitter at http://twitter.com/salestipaday.

Jeffrey Gitomer Tweets Relating to Social Media.

Twitter is not just freedom of speech, it's freedom of thought and freedom of expression. gitomer November 5, 2010 9:52:15 AM EDT via web

Wondering how to use (or better use) social media for sales success? Watch this webinar! http://bit.ly/socialmediaforsales October 27, 2010 11:05:41 AM EDT via Mobile Web

All bosses that are against social media are the ones who don't know how to use it. gitomer October 5, 2010 1:44:12 PM EDT via web

Too #many #hashtags #make #you #look #like a jack#ss. Pick one word that will lead people to you, like #sales, #loyalty, or #gitomer July 11, 2010 10:51:12 AM EDT via web

Yellow Pages only tells people where you are. Google tells you who you are, where you are, & how good you are – or are not. gitomer July 10, 2010 9:36:48 AM EDT via web

Social media is the new cold call, and you're still out there banging on doors. gitomer May 28, 2010 6:23:36 AM EDT via web

Your company won't let you use Facebook because management's heads are in the sand. gitomer May 28, 2010 3:41:07 AM EDT via web

You could put the words "up yours" in the middle of your brochure and no one would ever find them. gitomer April 13, 2010 4:21:44 PM EDT via web

Social media – the new cold call. Wanna play?
http://bit.ly/5ftvJN gitomer January 17, 2010 5:23:51 PM EST
via web

Business success. The well-prepared are most likely to
survive. The best-prepared are most likely to win. gitomer
July 28, 2009 6:30:10 PM EDT via web

The challenge with great quotes is: People see them at a
glance, don't realize their power, and fail to take action.
gitomer July 24, 2009 6:47:42 AM EDT via web

It's not just thinking – it's capturing your thoughts and turning
them into reality. What have you been thinking about?
Gitomer July 14, 2009 6:29:30 AM EDT via web

How to spend time in thought: Write your thoughts as you
come up with them. This way you preserve and clarify your
thinking. Gitomer July 14, 2009 6:27:19 AM EDT via web

TIME MANAGEMENT: You already know what to do, you're
just not doing it. gitomer May 4, 2009 8:32:15 AM EDT via web

When you have a choice of what to do – always do what you
will remember the most. Gitomer April 23, 2009 10:56:48 PM
EDT via web

"No brainers" are usually directed at people with no brains.
gitomer April 23, 2009 1:27:49 AM EDT

There are never enough happy days, even if every day is
happy. #gitomer 8:26 AM Dec 25th, 2010 via web

You don't have to "capture the spirit." You create spirit from
within, and keep it lit daily with your enthusiasm. gitomer
1:24 PM Dec 14th, 2010 via web

The world is not just small, it's instant.

JEFFREY GITOMER

YOUTUBE
BOOM!

The Difference Between Social Media and Business Social Media on YouTube.

YouTube provides the biggest opportunity for you to promote your name and your brand. Anyone in the world can find you and your information.

And it's FREE!

If you have a YouTube channel, go to the main page and see how many total views you have. If it's less than 1,000 you haven't provided enough opportunities for others to find you, or enough value for any kind of viral activity.

Let me share some YouTube opportunities with you:

- **Create a library of customer testimonials, tips, and ideas about your product that appear in no brochure.**

- **Record business philosophies that you have and want to share with others.**

- **Record your best idea of the week.**

- **Record your favorite customer of the week.**

- **Record your favorite restaurant in your city.**

You get the idea.

Your ability to broadcast on your own YouTube channel is limited only by your imagination and your allocated time. And did I mention, IT'S FREE!

Start with customer testimonial videos because they will lead you to more customers and you can pull them up when you're making a sales presentation to prove a point.

KEY POINT OF UNDERSTANDING: Keep all videos short and light. (One to four minutes is the ideal length.) Keep all videos fun and real. Make sure the videos that you post are an accurate representation of who you are in the business world, and what you believe to be true with your customers, your product, your company, and you.

And here's the best part: YouTube is FREE!

Free Git✗Bit... There is a specific action plan I follow to create impactful YouTube videos. If you'd like the list, visit http://www.gitomer.com and enter the words VIDEO PLAN in the GitBit box.

How to Get Lucky on YouTube.

By Julien Smith

In the seven years I have participated in social media, I've encountered a lot of success stories. Many are new businesses that couldn't have existed before.

The success happens because of email marketing, Twitter, blogs, and many other platforms. But none consistently surprise me like the success stories from YouTube.

YouTube is magic. Never before has any audience been found in one single "place." Ever. Never have more people been able to access information of all kinds. (I recently learned how to open any coconut in 30 seconds.) Never have more people been able to share what knowledge they do have, helping people grow, all for free.

On the other side of the coin are video producers. They have access to the simplest, easiest tools in the history of the world to give the population of YouTube whatever they need to know. Niche markets are created in YouTube daily, created by ad-hoc populations of information seekers (much like what Quora, another up-and-coming social site, does today). If users can't find it, they can become producers and get seen themselves.

In other words, YouTube is an entertainment and information marketplace. I know social networks well, but the ways people find to succeed on YouTube never cease to amaze me. There are hundreds, maybe thousands, of business models.

Because of YouTube, my friend Julie Angel (*SlamCamSpam* on YouTube or http://www.JulieAngel.com) has become one of the most published academics and documentary filmmakers in the world. Her videos started with footage she already had, but she has now compiled many millions of views. This has led to work with clients like Canon, Nokia, Native Instruments, Yota, and more.

Julie said she was impressed when she saw 90 views on her first video – after all, that's more than she'd get at a film festival.

Walt Ribeiro (http://www.ForOrchestra.com or *WaltRibeiro* on YouTube) is an entirely other kind of YouTube success story. In some ways, he's like a regular music teacher, teaching lessons to kids every day. But in other ways, he is totally new. Most music teachers have around 10 students a day, but Ribeiro has thousands, all for free. And because YouTube is "always open," he is also teaching people while he sleeps – at the same time working less (and making more) than most music teachers ever could. Further, he doesn't compete with other teachers, but instead, with magazines and other music publications.

Because YouTube features new highlights, and people want to watch new videos every day, there are always new stories like this. And when producers first get a taste of success, there is a good chance they learn how to take advantage of it to build something sustainable.

In fact, success on YouTube only has a little bit to do with luck. Some may come across it accidentally, but strategies do exist that help all kinds of people build an audience they can foster for years to come.

Here's how to build an audience on YouTube that you can foster for years to come:

START WITH WHAT YOU HAVE. No matter the social network, people who succeed get a leg up by using existing advantages they already have. Whether it be content or specialized knowledge, they never start from scratch, helping them get ahead of the pack.

Julie Angel had access to some of the top parkour specialists in the world – something most people would never be able to have. So her content is a natural winner in a YouTube market. Do you have this kind of access? Ask someone else what advantages you have, since you may take it for granted.

DON'T CREATE VIDEOS. CREATE SERIES OF VIDEOS. When you're teaching anything on YouTube, making it a series of short videos not only keeps people's attention, it also helps you have more views and chances for ads being clicked. The more viewers follow you through the content, the more they'll feel they've come to know you. And every time they click to a new video, there's a new chance for them to hit that Subscribe button, helping you communicate with them in the future.

USE EXISTING CONTENT. Don't start from nothing. Take advantage of any video you already have, or any content you've previously created or wanted to create. Use old ideas and recreate them in video format so that you can start quickly without getting overwhelmed by a need for new ideas.

USE SOCIAL PROOF. Do you have videos of yourself speaking in front of an audience, or where someone else is talking about your company instead of yourself? Testimonials and crowds display credibility without you having to say it yourself, helping you be seen as an authority in your field.

Walt Ribeiro used social proof in a different way. To help sponsors feel comfortable with his new media project, he quickly got one sponsor on board to show that other companies were already trusting him. This helped others get on board quicker, and at a higher sponsorship rate.

SCHEDULE YOUR SHOWS. Everyone has a website they visit in the morning before anything else, whether it be Facebook, a certain blog, or CNN.com. Help your audience by telling them when new shows will come out – then produce those shows in advance, so you won't end up editing late into the night (as I have done too many times).

BUILD YOURSELF AN ARMY. We wrote about building armies in the book *Trust Agents*, but the way some use it is extremely effective. They ask their fans directly: "Could you tell five friends about this video today?"

After you've built some trust with your audience, a direct request like this can be taken pretty seriously, leading to new subscribers or new viewers really quickly.

I've used this technique to great effect on my blog (http://www.InOverYourHead.net). After all, at the end of a video or post, people are looking for the next thing, so providing a call-to-action can be really helpful.

CHANGE YOUR BUSINESS MODEL. Once you're in the video business, your job is no longer just to make videos… but what that business becomes is up to you.

Are you selling sponsorships, or are you trying to get clients by showing your authority and value? Decide where the videos will help, or create multiple videos that speak to different segments of a market and see which ones take off.

When Julie Angel showed the incredible action videos she had made, with world-class parkour experts doing flips and jumping from one building to another, she showed that she was capable of producing great work without having to go through the usual routes. YouTube allowed her to connect and be messaged directly by whatever opportunity came by.

LISTEN TO COMMENTS. Comments on YouTube are known for being incendiary, yet every producer I spoke to said they were critical to the success of their project. Julie Angel confirms that each comment helps her understand where she went wrong in her videos, or what part viewers like best. They also help foster a community and build social proof, not to mention that the best comments can spark new ideas for future work.

FINALLY, HAVE A PLAN. But don't be afraid to make mistakes! Search "first video" on YouTube some time; you'll see horrible videos by people who have later become polished, funny, charming, and compelling. This is a natural process, but remember to keep that early authenticity to help you connect with your audience. People expect a certain vulnerability on YouTube, so trying to appear perfect will not go over well. Good luck!

Julien Smith is The New York Times bestselling co-author of Trust Agents. *He is a consultant and speaker who has been involved in online communities for over 15 years – from early BBSes and flashmobs to the social web as we know it today.*

Julien has long been on the cutting edge of web technology. He was one of the first Twitter users, and among the first people to use podcasting in 2004. He has since worked with and been interviewed by numerous media organizations such as CNN, CBC, CTV – and a bunch of others that don't start with the letter C. You can contact Julien at juliensmith@gmail.com.

What you do outside of social media will determine your fate inside of social media. If you're a sales rep in a business and you get to work on time and you meet your monthly quota and you make President's Club and you go home at six o'clock and you watch TV, answer emails, and prepare for the next day's sales calls, you will not do well in business social media.

JEFFREY GITOMER

THE GLUE!

BLOG. BLOG. BLOG.

Blogging is a huge part of the glue process that connects Facebook, LinkedIn, Twitter, and YouTube.

By posting consistent, valuable content and videos, your message becomes both searchable and relevant in your subject of expertise, and your desire to communicate valuable information to your audience of followers.

Blogs create attraction and thereby subscribers. And blogs have links to everywhere in the world, including social media pages.

Blogging is both fun and easy. It's also free. You choose the service.

As I have mentioned before, the first step is to register http://www.yourname.com. NOW. There are hundreds of places to do it. I'm choosing not to mention any of them on purpose.

If your name is taken, add the word "blog" to the end of your name. If it's still taken, use something creative at the front of your name, like "the great" or "I am" until you finally find one that is available. Use your name as the destination site for your blog.

Take a look at my blog. It's located at http://www.salesblog.com.

NOTE: How much content is there.

NOTE: How many videos are there.

NOTE: How many links are there.

NOTE: What's for sale.

ALSO NOTE: Its connectivity with my other social media outlets.

Here are 2.5 elements that your blog should contain:

1. **A biography and photos of you that are current.** Make it human and personal.

2. **A statement of value that reflects why you're blogging in the first place.**

2.5 **News, fun, insight, value, categories, specific information, humor, and other pass-on-able and subscribe-able information.**

I recommend you visit, subscribe to, and study the following blogs. They are examples of how successful business people and authors have created incredible blogs with substantial followings. I recommend them because I consider them valuable to me. I know they will be valuable examples to you.

Jeff Jarvis
www.buzzmachine.com

Jeff Jarvis is an author. His book, *What Would Google Do?* is a *New York Times* bestseller that you must own and read.

Buzzmachine is his incredible, well-written blog. (It better be! Jeff is a journalism professor.) It contains information on everything from Google to Jeff's prostate cancer episode.

Equally as important to note is what Jeff's blog has done to his Twitter page. With more then 60,000 followers, and appearing on more than 6,600 lists, Jeff Jarvis is the essence of value messaging that creates attraction and ultimately more followers. If you need any more authenticity, keep in mind that Jeff is a regular guest on the "Howard Stern" show.

Seth Godin
www.sethgodin.typepad.com

Seth Godin is an original. He is a blogger. He is an author. He is a speaker. And he is very well followed.

He has more than 60,000 followers, he appears on more than 6,500 lists, and he comments on just about everything in the world.

Seth is not just an author, he is not just a writer, he is not just a speaker, and he is certainly not just a tweeter. Seth Godin is a thinker – a world-class, leading thinker – who by blogging has attracted thousands of followers on Twitter. And just for the record, he has only tweeted 912 times.

His blog lists all of his books and links to them on his website, and contains over nine years of valuable, forwardable information.

Ali Edwards
www.aliedwards.com

Ali Edwards is a Life Artist, an author, and a speaker.

Ali is one of the world's most renowned designers and scrapbookers. She is also a mom.

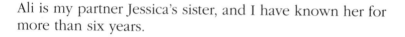

Ali is my partner Jessica's sister, and I have known her for more than six years.

Ali blogs about scrapbooking, design, life, family, autism, and children. She also sells sponsor space on her blog that helps support her family and her desire to continue in her chosen field.

Her blog is beyond excellent. It has thousands of loyal followers. She receives hundreds (sometimes thousands) of comments every day. And even though she has a ton of sponsors on her blog, they still appear tastefully.

To feature (and reward) her sponsors, Ali posts giveaways of their products. Those giveaways create thousands of responses and leads for the sponsors and an ability for the sponsor to witness the power of Ali's blog.

NOTE WELL: If you think you can't make a solid living by blogging, take a real close look at Ali Edwards. She is a classic living example of how family, quality, and value can manifest itself into dollars.

The Glue Process.

Throughout this book, there have been mentions of the elements outside business social media that create additional attraction to the elements inside business social media.

I have referred to them as "glue."

Anything you do in your business career creates attraction toward social media if you do it right.

You give a speech, and at the end of the speech you ask people to follow you. If they liked your speech, they will.

The biggest glue elements require the most work:

- **Your personal website.**
- **Your weekly e-zine.**
- **Your blog.**

If you decide to write on a daily basis, you can create a lot of attraction through blogging.

If you decide to send a weekly value message to each of your customers and prospects, you can create a lot of attraction through an e-zine.

I do both.

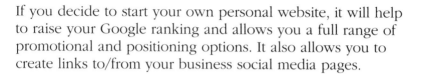

If you decide to start your own personal website, it will help to raise your Google ranking and allows you a full range of promotional and positioning options. It also allows you to create links to/from your business social media pages.

Other glue elements that I use are my public seminars, my weekly column that appears in newspapers, my books, my other video products, and (most important) mother Google. Google creates a directional beacon toward everything I have and everything I do.

I am searchable, I am findable, and I am approachable.

I use the term *glue* because it's sticky and it holds things together. I don't just have a business Facebook page, I don't just have a Twitter account, I don't just have LinkedIn connections, I don't just have a YouTube channel – I have a cohesive game plan to connect one to the other, and when combined with several outside elements, it creates major momentum toward me that grows daily.

Slow at first, it requires, no, it actually demands, consistency. After you develop the discipline and create the elements, you can manufacture your own glue. You decide whether you want a small tube or a 55-gallon drum.

Personally I want to be in the drum business.

The Power of Your Email Magazine.

At the beginning of 2001, unaware our world would change on September 11th, we called 1,000 of our customers and asked them for email addresses so we could send them my weekly column. We were fortunate enough to gather 21,000 names.

NOTE: It was a time when email addresses were not as closely guarded as they were today.

ALSO NOTE: I had a reputation as an author and a following from my weekly column.

We created an email list and sent my weekly column out. I asked my brother Josh to create the first design of my email magazine. And in spite of the events of 9/11, I sent issue one of *Sales Caffeine* in November 2001.

The response was immediate, the response was positive, and the response blew me away. People began forwarding my email magazine to others, who would then subscribe.

One week we tried selling one of my books and immediately sold hundreds. So we decided to combine the weekly value message with an offer to sell.

Every week, my email magazine:

- **Presents a consistent message.**
- **Contains valuable information.**
- **Attracts new subscribers.**
- **Is a money-maker.**

From my e-zine, people buy books, tickets to public seminars, and special offers. They're willing to take advantage of my learning materials because they can relate to and appreciate my free materials of value.

Well into our ninth year, our active list now contains more than 300,000 subscribers.

Sales Caffeine has gone through six major design changes and will no doubt undergo more. It now links to all my social media pages. I now videotape my weekly column, so you can both read and watch the value message. I post a weekly sales rant that is housed on YouTube. And there are more than 20 links in each issue that will lead you to read more, learn more, or buy more.

My email magazine has become the fulcrum point of my business. It has created an opportunity for me to stay in front of, and stay top of mind to, all my customers. Internally, it's gone from a part-time position to a full-time position.

PLEASE: Use my email magazine as a model for your own.

NOTE WELL: I consider my email mailing list my single most valuable business asset.

Creating a weekly value message that reaches every one of your customers and prospects is not an option in today's business world. It's a marketing tool, a branding tool, a communication tool, and a money tool. And it's a vital element of glue in your business social media campaign.

SOCIAL BOOM!

Got Value?

Value is a complex word, but you better dissect and understand its complexity because value is at the heart of your business social media challenge, opportunity, and path to success.

I post value updates on Facebook, I have attracted thousands of LinkedIn followers because of value, I tweet value, and I post value videos on YouTube.

REALITY: Value must be perceived as such by the recipient, or it has none. If you think it's valuable and your connections think it is not valuable, then *delete* will overpower *forward* or *share*.

CHALLENGE: Put yourself in the shoes, and in the chair, and in the mind of your connections. Read whatever it is you wrote aloud, and ask yourself: *How will I use this to learn? How will I use this to earn? How will I use this to better my business? How will I use this to better myself? How will I use this to better my life?*

If those questions cannot be answered in a positive manner, you have not achieved value in the mind of your connections, and your business social media outreach will suffer accordingly.

GOOD NEWS: Value is rare. Because I'm a value provider, I study value. And because I'm in a market with many other authors, speakers, writers, publishers, and business people, I study their value. I get their emails, I go to their websites, and I read their offerings – mostly followed by the delete key.

Oh, they offer stuff that they believe to be valuable, but in the end it's an exchange they're hoping for. Their perceived value for your money. Big mistake.

HERE IS MY SECRET: I put myself in front of people that can say yes to me, and I deliver value first.

Your messages of value have to be genuine, authentic, and without an offer to buy. Your messages of value must be transparent, and without expectation of return or response.

When your followers and your connections realize that you offer genuine help, and that your messages have real-world value, they will begin to buy from you because they believe the rest of what you offer also has value. Value to them.

I see all kinds of lessons, I see all kinds of classes, I see all kinds of downloads, and I see all kinds of offers about how to win at, how to build up, and how to monetize social media. But I rarely see the word "value" in those messages. And I NEVER see valuable information offered before payment is rendered.

But value isn't a deep, dark secret. In fact, I don't think there's anything more obvious on the planet! If you give value to someone without any obligation or expectation, they will like it, connect with it, tell others, and want more – *the very essence of business social media.*

Value first, connections second, money third. Money is not the motive, it's the by-product and the report card for doing the right thing *with value.*

Value first, connections second, money third. Money is not the motive, it's the by-product and the report card for doing the right thing with value.

JEFFREY GITOMER

Help, I Want to Write, But I Don't Know How!

The core process of business social media is writing. Every aspect of Facebook, LinkedIn, Twitter, and YouTube requires writing. Clear, concise, compelling writing.

Over the past 15 years, I have become a successful writer. Many of you aspire to do the same. Or at least to be a better writer.

I often get the following calls for writing help:

"How do I write like you?"

"I'm not a very good writer."

"I sit down to write and nothing comes out."

I can't teach you "how to write." Or "how to write better." I can share with you how I write, and you can take it from there.

Everyone needs to (learn to) write in a more compelling manner. Clear, concise, compelling writing is a rarity in our world. Email and text messaging has helped with clear and concise, but it has taken "compelling" out of the formula.

Facebook, LinkedIn, Twitter, YouTube, e-zines, and blogs have put compelling back in.

I'm sharing my personal writing habits and methods on the next few pages because I believe they will help you better understand writing and become a better writer.

Here are the writing strategies I implement daily. These are the lessons I've learned after writing 1,000 weekly columns and 11 books:

I write like I think. I write like I talk. The thoughts I write are a silent extension of what I would have said if I were speaking aloud. That's why I read aloud when I edit. I want my writing to sound like I'm talking. I will often get a letter or email that says, "I felt like you were talking to me as I was reading" or "I felt like you were standing right there." That's because I "write" in "speak."

I write anywhere, anytime. I don't need a space or a place. I just need an idea or a thought. I write when an idea strikes. If I'm not near a computer, I find any scrap of paper or napkin I can get my hands on – the object is to capture the idea or thought the moment it pops into your mind. You will *never* remember it later.

I collect ideas. I collect thoughts. I have hundreds of them. When I want to write about something or have a deadline, I select one of my ideas and expand on it.

When I get the idea, I stretch it. I write everything that comes to mind. All of the thoughts, phrases, or words I can think of. I just brain dump until it's all out. I may edit a few things when I'm done, but I write in a flurry because ideas are fleeting and thoughts are even more fleeting. In 17 years of writing, the one thing I have found to be most true is that thoughts will leave your head if you don't write them down at once.

I write from my own experience. I don't need research statistics to back up a thought or a concept. Either it happened to me, or I believe it to be true based on my personal experience. Statistics lie. I don't.

When I write a column or a chapter, I stick to one subject, thought, or theme. This creates an in-depth look and forces me to look way beyond the norm and create new ideas for worn-out methods and conventional thinking.

I write to convey the value of my message in a clear and actionable way. I want to make certain that my message is transferrable and actionable on the part of the reader. If the reader considers my words, thoughts, and ideas valuable, they will take immediate action, AND share my words, thoughts, and ideas with others.

I don't care about grammar. I write so that the reader can "get it." I care about how it sounds when it's read, and how it looks when you read it, not what some silly rule says. I put hyphens and apostrophes where they don't belong, so that the reader has an easy time following the flow and understand the thought.

I care about structure and flow. I want one thought to flow to another. Where it doesn't or can't, I make (structure) a list of things. The lists flow from top to bottom.

I rely on spell checker and keep on writing until I complete the thought. I never stop writing to "fix" something until the thought I'm writing is complete. Spelling and writing are mutually exclusive. If you stop to spell, you lose thought flow and momentum. You can always check your spelling. You can't always retain the thought or flow.

My writing voice is not PC. If I waste time with "his or her," I lose my thought. I don't mean to be insulting, I'm just writing in my voice. It's how I grew up. It's the same voice as all the early books I read, and continue to read. **NOTE WELL:** It's a *message* and a *thought*; it's an *idea* or a *strategy* – not a *gender*.

I write in the male gender because I'm a male. I never mean to offend anyone. I'm trying to make points, generate new thinking, and help people succeed. That advice knows no gender. Read *between* the pronouns. Don't get hung up on them.

I do not include myself with the reader. I separate myself from the reader with pronouns. I say "you," "your," "they," "he," "she," "it," or "the." NEVER "we" or "our." I talk to the reader, but never include myself in the thought. NOT, "We all know…" Rather, "You know." NOT, "Our thoughts tell us…" Rather, "Your thoughts tell you…."

I break the rules of traditional writing, grammar, and punctuation. Grammar teachers wouldn't give me a passing grade. Who cares? I've sold a million books. How many have they sold?

I edit when I finish, but I edit better a day later. Editing is revealing. It tells you what you were thinking at the moment you wrote it. Editing a day later also reveals, "What was I thinking when I wrote this?" My editing secret is that I read aloud when I edit. And I ask others to edit when I think I'm finished. Both of these secrets make my writing twice as powerful.

I end my lists with .5 rather than a whole number, for 2.5 basic reasons.

1. The .5 statement at the end of each list I make is the glue that binds the rest of the list.

2. Ending this way makes me think deeper and on a higher level about the subject. The .5 is where I can add philosophy, humor, challenge, and a final call to action.

2.5 It makes my lists different from all other lists. It brands me, and sets me apart from all other list makers (except for the few that copy me).

I love to write. This may be the biggest secret of writing with passion and clarity. I believe loving it makes the thoughts flow deeper and more consistently. I believe loving it makes me consider "long-term legacy" as well as "short-term impact." I believe my love of writing makes me a more complete writer. Content becomes more relevant, and pride of authorship shows through in every sentence.

I write with authority. I'm emphatic and declarative. If you read my thoughts, you have no doubt about what I'm saying or how I feel about it.

I just counted personal pronouns. The word "I" appears here more than 90 times. A record. I use first person singular sparingly. If you're a regular reader, you know I avoid first person plural (we, our) like the plague. It sucks the power out of my writing. And it drains the impact by lowering the value of the writer. When you write, you're the authority. Your reader is probably not. Don't include yourself with them.

Less about me and more about your writing skills. Here are 5.5 things you can do to improve your skills today:

1. **Just sit down and write something. Every day.**

2. **Save your best thoughts and ideas the second they occur. Not on a pad of paper or a diary. ON A COMPUTER. Where you can reread it, expand it, and edit it.**

3. **Write it like you would say it.**

4. **Make sure your thoughts are simple, easy to understand, and complete.**

5. **Edit early and often.**

5.5 **Remember that you're writing for the reader AND yourself.**

To see if you're on the right track as you edit your writing, ask yourself these questions:

- Where's the impact?

- Where's the meat?

- Where's the point?

- Where's the hook?

- Where's the value?

- Is it compelling?

- Will the reader want to read it all?

- Will the reader think as a result of this writing?

- Will the reader act as a result of this writing?

- Will the reader tell others to read it?

- Will the reader send this writing to others?

- Will the reader post a comment?

- Will the reader want more of this?

IMPORTANT: These rules and strategies are not just for business social media, they're for writing. And business social media is just a PART of writing. Writing is integral to your success and plays an important role in your earnings.

I REPEAT: Every aspect of business social media has at its core: writing. Learn to write by writing every day.

Free Git✗Bit... Want to know the writers who positively influenced me? Go to http://www.gitomer.com and enter the words AYN RAND in the GitBit box.

The Four Rules of Word-of-Mouth Marketing.

By Andy Sernovitz

HERE'S THE BIG NEWS: It's not social MEDIA. It's SOCIAL media. It's about real people and the conversations they have.

That's what we call word of mouth – and that's the thing that changes your business forever.

Social media is an incredible tool to help word of mouth. It enables word of mouth to go farther, faster, and to more people. But word of mouth is the goal, social media is the tool.

Word of mouth is about encouraging people to talk about you. It's about earning the respect and recommendation of your customers. It's about turning customers into fans and employees into evangelists.

Here are the rules for how to successfully do it:

Rule #1: Be Interesting.

Nobody talks about boring companies, boring products, or boring ads. If you want people to talk about you, you've got to do something special. Anything. If you are boring, you'll never get a moment of conversation. Your word of mouth will fall flat on its face. (Actually, it will just fade away, unnoticed.)

Before you run an ad, before you launch a product, before you put something new on the menu, ask the magic question: *Would anyone tell a friend about this?*

Take a trick from the Chicago Bagel Authority's 56 bizarrely named sandwiches, like the Hoosier Daddy and the Muenster Mash. Or the seven-inch-high corned beef sandwiches at New York's famous Carnegie Deli. It would still be the best corned beef sandwich in the world if it were a normal size. But its insane mass guarantees that hundreds of tourists leave the restaurant every day to spread the word about one of the greatest sights in the Big Apple.

There are probably hundreds of shoeshine stands in New York City. But everybody goes to Eddie's in Grand Central Station. They tell their friends to make a special trip to go there (passing plenty of other good shoeshine stands on the way). Why? Eddie's has huge, comfy, old-fashioned, red leather easy chairs to sit in. You feel like a king when you sit back and enjoy a few minutes of peace in those chairs at the end of the day.

Give people a reason to talk about you.

And please, I beg you, stop for a minute before you buy more advertising. Think about how much money you are about to spend. Think about how fast you, and everyone else in the world, flip past hundreds of ads without even noticing them. Don't run another ad unless it is truly worth talking about.

Rule #2: Make It Easy.

Word of mouth is lazy. You've got to help it along if you expect it to go anywhere.

You need to do two things: Find a super-simple message and help people share it.

Start with a topic that anyone can remember. Something like, "Our software doesn't crash," or "They have chocolate cream cheese!" or "They give you snacks while you're waiting for a table," or "Stupid name, but it sure does work." (Anything longer than a sentence is too much. It'll get forgotten or mangled.)

We all think of Steve Jobs as the greatest computer marketer who ever lived. So what did he do when he returned to Apple in 1996 with the mission of reviving a stumbling company? Did he talk about great software? Stable operating systems? No.

Jobs' great marketing insight was pink and purple computers.

It got everyone talking. It restarted positive word of mouth about the company. Everyone told a friend because they had a simple topic of conversation that was interesting to share. And when people heard about the cute computers, they were ready to take another look at the more important features.

Once you've got your big word-of-mouth idea, find a bunch of ways to make it easier to spread. There are countless ways to make your ideas portable. A special announcement on a website or brochure is stuck in place. Put it in an email, though, and it's in motion.

Rule #3: Make People Happy.

Happy customers are your greatest advertisers.

Thrill them. Create amazing products. Provide excellent service. Go the extra mile. Make the experience remarkable.

Fix problems, too. Make sure the work you do gets people energized, excited, and eager to tell a friend.

When people like you, they share you with their friends. They want to help you, they want to support your business, and they want their friends to enjoy what you offer. You will get more word of mouth from making people happy than anything else you could possibly do.

Let's look at one of the great mysteries of the modern age. In 1999, why did 60,000 people drive their plain Saturn sedans to Spring Hill, Tennessee, to meet the people who made them? What car could possibly be less interesting than a Saturn?

The annual Saturn Homecoming was a great word-of-mouth marketing strategy. But it wouldn't have worked if people didn't trust and respect Saturn. People really liked the company. They liked its attitude. They felt taken care of by the nice salespeople and the company's no-haggle concept. And they were amazed when they got a friendly note twice a year with instructions on how to adjust the clock for daylight-saving time.

So they told their friends, thereby supporting the company that supported them.

Let's look at another great mystery of the modern age. Why do some people like Target so much? This I won't attempt to explain, but I'm not the only guy who, while on vacation, has been taken to visit a Target that looks exactly like the one we have at home. (Aargh.)

Target makes my wife happy in a way that would threaten a less manly man. But they have some stylish stuff. Decent prices. Clean stores. A fun attitude.

And she talks to everyone about it.

Rule #4: Earn Trust and Respect.

If you don't have respect, you don't get good word of mouth.

Nobody talks positively about a company that they don't trust or like. Nobody puts their name on the line for a company that will embarrass them in front of their friends.

Always be an honorable company. Make ethics part of everything you do. Be good to your customers. Talk to them. Fulfill their needs. Make people proud to tell your story to everyone they know.

Southwest Airlines is one of the most trusted brands in the world. It treats its customers well, with few hassles and a great attitude. It treats its employees well, with stable jobs, a no-layoff policy, and decent pay. People like Southwest. People like the company so much that they sent cash to the airline after 9/11 to help it out.

Lots of people are spreading great word of mouth about Southwest. Does anyone have anything good to say about most other airlines?

Every company can be nicer, and every employee can work to make his or her company a little better to its customers.

My bank offers pretty much the same services as every other bank. But they are really nice. Really, really nice. Tom and Abby remember my name and my wife's name. They even remember my baby's name, and she doesn't do much banking.

I banked at one of the top three banks for 10 years, and at one time my company had more than $1 million on deposit. I could barely get them to cash a check or take my calls. And after a while, the random, punitive fees started to eat away any respect I had for this venerable institution.

Negative word of mouth from people like me has sent a whole lot of money to banks that treat people better.

YOU ONLY HAVE TWO CHOICES: You can be special enough that people want to talk about you. Or you can buy advertising. I think that advertising is the cost of being boring.

Making a good product isn't good enough anymore. Everyone does that these days. Because being good is different than being worth talking about.

Is your product worth talking about? Really? Be honest. If it's not, now is the time to raise the bar, change the game, and make it buzzworthy.

If you are not creating stuff that makes you wake up every day and shout, "I love what I do and I'm dying to tell you about it!" then I compel you to make it wonderful, outrageous, purple, delicious, smelly, goofy, life-saving, amazing, or deeply meaningful.

You'll be glad you did. It's more fun to work at (or own) a company that people love to talk about.

Andy Sernovitz teaches word-of-mouth marketing. He is CEO of GasPedal, a word-of-mouth consulting company, and SocialMedia.org, the community for heads of social media at the world's greatest brands. He taught Word-of-Mouth Marketing at Northwestern University and Internet Entrepreneurship at the Wharton School of Business, ran a business incubator, and started half a dozen companies. He created the Word of Mouth Marketing Association and the Association for Interactive Marketing.

You can visit his amazing blog called "Damn I Wish I'd Thought of That" at http://www.damniwish.com.

Social Media for Business.
A Careerist's Perspective.

By Shar Govindan

It is not uncommon to find a business professional with over 500+ contacts on LinkedIn with only a few hundred friends on Facebook and vice versa. There are several thousand other micro-community sites targeted to serve professionals of a particular industry unknown to the general public.

Internet junkies tend to create an account on every popular social media site but often have a favorite.

Every site offers addictive features to their active users. Smart phones add fuel to the fire by offering free applications enabled to get instant updates. Social Media Addicts Anonymous groups are becoming increasingly popular and ironically users may seek therapy through communication tools offered by the same site. It is a little known fact that some companies hire psychologists to help design a system that will increase their website usage.

The fundamental differentiator is what features someone likes to use given the plethora of tools being introduced and improved on the Internet every day. It is as simple as why we like certain types of ads on TV or radio over others.

Another compelling reason to join is if the site is recommended by a friend, family member, or colleague. The power of word of mouth, the lifeline on which most businesses thrive or vanish, is the strongest and purest of all types of marketing.

There appears to be a clear divide between people who primarily use social media for personal use and those who use it for professional use. And each group may wonder what tangible benefit the other type provides over theirs.

Many employers research a potential recruit's "personal" profile page on the Internet as part of their background check process. Limited knowledge on how to set up the ever-changing privacy controls could expose job seekers to embarrassing details, photos, and information that they would normally not want to share with an interviewer.

Existing employees are no safer. Stories about people getting fired for complaining online about their workplace or boss is everyday news! Therefore, every social media type could be construed as a business one with serious consequences.

On the flip side, this is great news for people who smartly invest the time to showcase their online profile and stay up to date on the trends and news related to their job industry.

There is a team of marketing folks behind each large website having numerous meetings every day, brainstorming ideas on how to get our attention. Through our "selective hearing" abilities, we ignore the thought that all sites are aimed at generating revenue through increased Internet traffic – either via advertisements or subscription.

We can turn the tables on these commercial sites and enhance personal branding and marketability by learning the secrets of the pros.

I am not referring to a magic pill for a weight loss program that will help you lose 45 pounds in 30 days or how you can get a second book for free if you call within the next 15 minutes by paying separate shipping & handling. This is the real deal – it's an insight into how you are able to take advantage of the hidden opportunities and say thanks very much to the sponsors of Internet content.

Here are some of the ways power users create a clear advantage for themselves by harnessing the online opportunities:

A PROFESSIONAL PROFILE. This is more than just an online resume. In addition to providing an executive summary, education, experience and professional memberships, business users are able to solicit recommendations from colleagues, managers, customers, and industrial contacts. Having multiple recommendations from industrially recognized experts adds considerable credibility.

A PROFESSIONAL PHOTO. Get yourself a business head shot or portfolio from a local photo studio. This won't be cheap, but is a good investment. Many photographers allow you to try different attires and some even recommend makeup artists (even for men!) who specialize in giving you a "photogenic" look. The photo session can be at a studio or in a business setting like a conference room, your office, or beside your private jet.

NEWS FEEDS. Several sites allow you to subscribe to discussion topics, podcasts, or news sections of interest. You have the ability to customize your browser or configure your inbox to receive news articles as they are created. This saves time and allows you to track the information you actually care about.

NETWORK, NETWORK, AND NETWORK. As the saying goes, who you know is more important than what you know. Don't hesitate to send a connection request to a business associate.

Also, don't send too many unsolicited networking requests. The system may flag you as a spammer. Mastering the art of networking is highly rewarding. Choose who you want to be associated with and ask someone you both know in common to introduce you if necessary. It is also polite to send the person of interest a message before sending an invite to connect.

TRAVEL CONNECTIONS. This is the next closest thing to having a global tracking device embedded in your tooth (a new technology used by some pet owners). On a serious note, publishing a travel itinerary allows professionals to network in addition to their business trip's primary purpose. For example, tools can automatically notify business acquaintances living in different states that they may be in the same airport terminal on a certain time and day using their connecting flight information.

CREATE YOUR OWN COMMUNITY OR JOIN AN EXISTING ONE.
Most sites have "interest groups" that allow the discussion of relevant topics. This is a popular way to meet new people and network. Posting useful information or discussing a hot button topic like latest technologies or laws/regulations affecting them is a great way to have an interesting conversation.

You have the option to create your own website with the ability to post your profile, blog, post to Facebook, link to YouTube, tweet directly, subscribe to news feeds and e-zines from your favorite websites automatically, or pick a social media site that allows integration with other websites.

In other words, you can live on the Internet on a free or rental property, or own your own house.

The latest trend is the growing number of "niche" sites that target a very specific group of professionals. These portals are often created by a leading industrial organization or vendor.

For example, there may be a site just for civil engineers, offering a forum, news, yellow pages, classifieds, chat, blogs, articles, books & DVDs, jobs, contests, and social networking opportunities relevant to their industry.

Being able to network within a specific community with common interests delivers incredible value. Professionals are able to discuss ideas, solve problems, recommend books, prepare for certifications, and network without having to go to a conference or meeting.

Business social media is gaining popularity and has also attracted scammers looking to make a quick buck. Since most professionals are wary of giving their bank information to help "Mrs. Mogabu Dobova, the widow of a former president from a foreign country" wire transfer $15 million, there appears to be new ways that one has to watch out for.

A few months ago, I got a phone call from a "Who's who" with the same name as a famous educational institution. The lady wanted to interview me after reading all my professional achievements on a social media site. After asking a series of journalist sounding questions and appearing genuinely interested on my achievements, stroking my ego along the conversation, she declared I am now eligible to appear in their exclusive who's who directory and requested my photograph.

In addition to this VIP listing, I would also receive a certificate, an airline companion ticket, and special flyers. All that the lady wanted in exchange was my credit card information for processing this listing, a whopping $1,100 for Platinum listing. Not too bad for a 30-minute phone call and totally legitimate (loophole) proposal because it was for a directory listing. Sensing my hesitation, I was offered five different pricing options all the way down to $50.

(A quick online search revealed that this company had scammed innocent professionals who had a tough time getting their money back. They also had no affiliation to the educational institution and simply chose their name to sound credible.)

Another popular scam is companies that work with job seekers promising them exclusive job listings that are not listed anywhere else for a fee. It is always a good idea to do background research on "special" offers.

As social media sites compete to revolutionize our experience on the web and increase signups, they also offer the perfect platform for individuals and companies to become popular within their industrial segment. Each of these sites offers an inexpensive and efficient way to be the marketing guru for your most important brand, Y-O-U!

Shar Govindan works as the global technical director for an engineering software company based in Texas. He has an MS in Environmental Engineering from the University of Connecticut. He has authored several technical articles and is a frequent presenter at engineering, GIS, and CAD conferences. Shar has been an early adopter of several social media sites and uses them to professionally network every day.

As a hobby, Shar created his first community site in 1995 and has designed several hundred websites since then.

Visit Shar's LinkedIn profile at http://www.linkedin.com/in/ sharavan.

Are You an Employee or a Person?

Business social media is not just an opportunity. It's also an obstacle. Many businesses have rules, regulations, policies, and barriers that may preclude you from using any and all forms of social media that include their business name.

ACTION: Continue as an employee, but divorce yourself from the company as a person. There are no rules that preclude you from participating in any of the social media as a *human being*.

If you're in banking, insurance, pharmaceuticals, or any other business that has a legal department that begins with the word no and ends with with the word no, then take the business name out of everything you do.

You can tweet about, and you can blog about, and you can Facebook about aspects of your relationship that customers and prospects deem significant, never mentioning the name of your company, or your affiliation with it.

There is no rule against telling people the best place to take a weekend vacation, how to keep your front yard safe, how to reduce costs of heating and air conditioning in your home, or your personal philosophies and insights about life.

NOTE WELL: Leave out offers to buy.

Rather, create opportunities that will allow you to connect and opportunities to get together and meet. A seminar, a networking event, even a party.

Make the information valuable, and I guarantee it will get forwarded. Business social media is an opportunity for you to build your personal brand, build personal awareness, build your personal network, and build your personal reputation.

Yes, it takes a little chutzpah, but it will save you the embarrassment, and loss of ground, of not doing it at all.

CONSIDER THIS: Suppose you left your job tomorrow, or got laid off, or got fired. The first thing your prospective new employer is going to do when considering you for a position is check your online status and your Google ranking.

In today's employment world, you don't even need a resume because your Google rank, your social media presence, and your overall online presence speaks way louder than what your high school gym teacher (from 20 years ago) thinks of you.

There is a big difference between references and reputation.

And if you're in sales, the only people I am going to call for a reference are your prior customers.

FINAL PIECE OF ADVICE: If you're frustrated by what you can't do, start doing what you can do.

Your (Personal) Business Social Media Game Plan.

Regardless of where you are in the construction or operation of your business social media outreach, I'm asking you to relook at and rethink about the process because the odds are you started it with the wrong motive: money and sales.

In regard to your business Facebook page, your Twitter account, your LinkedIn connections, and your YouTube channel – ask yourself these questions (for each of the four individually):

- **What am I hoping to achieve?**
- **Who am I wanting to attract, engage, and connect with?**
- **Who will help me design?**
- **Who will help me launch?**
- **Who will help me post?**
- **Who will be in charge of this process short term?**
- **Who will be in charge of this process long term?**
- **Do I need professional help?**
- **How much time am I willing to allocate each day?**
- **How often am I committing to update?**
- **What type of value messaging am I going to offer?**

The answers to these questions (written down) will create both structure and architecture for your entire business social media game plan. It will also determine your strategy for attracting, engaging, and connecting.

Lucky for you, most people started a Facebook page because their neighbor did or one of their friends did. Don't do that. Start (or restart) your business social media outreach with purpose, plan, and design. And start (or restart) it with an understanding of what you want to achieve. Not just a goal to launch, but also a goal to attract, a goal to engage, a goal to connect, and a goal for what you want the OUTCOME to be.

Whatever you do, do not follow the ill-fated, "Begin with the end in mind." A more bogus, meaningless statement has never been written to the world business population.

It should say, "Begin with the outcome defined."

If you don't begin *knowing what you want to achieve,* and *how you intend to achieve it,* then don't begin.

Business social media is far different from, and far more powerful than, social media. Business social media will allow you to keep existing customers loyal, attract new customers, build your reputation, and create more brand awareness than you could ever do with a full page ad every week in *Time* magazine, or a full page ad every Sunday in *The New York Times*.

MATH: Those ads will cost you millions of dollars a year, and guarantee you NOTHING. Business social media is free, and a million times more powerful, more authentic, and more valuable.

And if done correctly, business social media puts you in direct one-on-one contact with paying customers. That's a game plan you can take to the bank.

Ace of Sales Is
Social Media Ready.

There is a sales tool that will immediately link you and allow you to post on Facebook, Twitter, and LinkedIn. It's called Ace of Sales. And it's the only tool of its kind. It's located conveniently at http://www.aceofsales.com, and business social media is only a small portion of what Ace of Sales can do to help you make a sale.

Ace of Sales contains social media glue and sales glue:

- It will import all your contacts from Outlook in about three minutes.

- It has customizable emails so that your emails don't look like anyone else's emails.

- It has the ability to send a birthday card, thank-you note, or a post card just to say, "Hi."

- It has an e-zine template that will allow you to stay in touch with a value message to every customer, every week.

- It can be used with any CRM.

- It will allow you to create a full-blown sales campaign for any individual client or prospect.

Ace of Sales also contains more than 100 of my sales training vignettes. You'll have the opportunity to learn from my short, how-to video clips about dealing with any sales scenario in the sales cycle, whether you're online or face-to-face.

THE DEAL: The first 45 days of your Ace of sales subscription is free when you use the promo code: SOCIALBOOM. It will also allow you to send two free cards. (I recommend that you send one to yourself.)

When you see how easy this software is to use, and when you see how impactful your emails and correspondences are, you will wonder why it only costs $20 a month to subscribe. (There is a small charge to send the cards and the email magazine.)

The social media advantage that you have with your Ace of Sales home page puts everything within one click and allows you to see tweets, postings, and connections in real time. Thousands of people are on it. Be one of them.

ASK YOURSELF THIS AMUSING, YET POWERFUL QUESTION: Do you want to be an Ace of Database, an Ace of Social Media, and an Ace of Sales?

Jeffrey Gitomer's
ACE of SALES™

Formula for Business Social Media Success: Attract People, Engage People, Connect People.

The best way to accomplish all three elements of this formula is with value.

Everyone wants to know if there is a secret formula for business social media success and the answer is yes. The formula is actually a process. You may not like the formula because it requires work. Hard work. But I can promise you will like the monetary rewards that result from the hard work.

After you have created all your business social media pages and accounts, you have to make a beginning. The beginning deals with the word attraction.

What is attractive about you? Or better stated *what have you done in your past to ensure that you can attract in the present and in the future?*

After you attract, you must engage.

Your ability to engage is based on your expertise, your ideas, your wisdom, your mastery of a single subject, and even your humor. But whatever it is, when you have attracted someone, you then have the (huge) opportunity in business social media to engage them.

PICTURE THIS: You're at a global networking event. There are hundreds of millions of people in attendance. Your job is to engage your fair share.

If you have attracted them properly, and you have engaged them intellectually, or even monetarily (as a potential sale), then and only then is it possible that they'll connect with you.

You can attract, and you can engage, but if the messages aren't right, or the feeling of value is missing, they will *disengage* and leave your page or your site without connecting with you.

NOTE WELL: Connections are the basis for your success, and they're also the foundation for your growth. Not simply telling others, but remaining your connection. That's why this entire book stresses the word *consistency.*

I'm not going to wait around for you to post every month, but I'll eagerly anticipate your message that I'm attracted to and engaged by every week.

Attract. Engage. Connect.

There is one element that makes this formula work beyond all expectations. That element is the word *value.* Not just the word, rather the actions and the words you put into the value creation process.

Attract with hope, offer a message of value, engage with perceived value, and connect with quantifiable value. Now the formula is complete. Attract, engage, and connect with value.

The formula for business social media success:

Attract people
Engage people
Connect people

The best way to accomplish all three is with value.

JEFFREY GITOMER

I Can Help You Personally in Your Quest for Social BOOM!

Many companies (maybe yours) want to move ahead, but are uncertain of the right game plan, much less the right thing to post.

I can help you.

Many companies (maybe yours) want to create or recreate policies regarding the use of and participation in business social media.

I can help you.

I can consult with you, I can create game plans for you, I can help create your guidelines for use, and I can do a customized, personalized, seminar for any number of people in your company. I can help create and generate individual business social media success.

Please contact my office of friendly, helpful people.

Jeffrey Gitomer
704-333-1112

This Book Will Never End...

I have created a business social media online community. Join the discussion at http://www.BusinessSocialMedia.com.

The sites gives you and everyone else in the world, a chance to contribute ideas, ask questions, and share stories of achievement. It contains answers, updates, and new developments to help you gain greater exposure and success.

The site contains discussion groups with ongoing threads designed to help you gain more successful business social media outcomes.

Business social media evolves every day, and it is my goal and intension to keep this information current through an online meeting and discussion place.

Please participate.
Please share ideas.
Please ask questions.

Jeffrey Gitomer
Chief Executive Salesman

AUTHOR. Jeffrey is the author of *The New York Times* best sellers *The Sales Bible*, *The Little Red Book of Selling*, *The Little Black Book of Connections*, and *The Little Gold Book of YES! Attitude*. All of his books have been number one best sellers on Amazon. com. Jeffrey's books have sold millions of copies worldwide.

IN FRONT OF MILLIONS OF READERS EVERY WEEK. Jeffrey's syndicated column *Sales Moves* appears in scores of business journals and newspapers in the United States and Europe, and is read by more than four million people every week.

SALES CAFFEINE. Jeffrey's weekly e-zine, *Sales Caffeine*, is a sales wake-up call delivered every Tuesday morning to more than 500,000 subscribers worldwide, free of charge. *Sales Caffeine* allows Jeffrey to communicate valuable sales information, strategies, and answers to sales professionals on a timely basis. To sign up, or for more information, visit http://www.salescaffeine.com.

MORE THAN 100 PRESENTATIONS A YEAR. Jeffrey gives public and corporate seminars, runs annual sales meetings, and conducts live and Internet training programs on selling, customer loyalty, and personal development.

SALES ASSESSMENT ONLINE. The world's first customized sales assessment, renamed a "successment," will judge your selling skill level in 12 critical areas of sales knowledge and give you a diagnostic report that includes 50 mini sales lessons. This amazing tool will help you rate your sales abilities and explain your opportunities for sales growth. This program is aptly named KnowSuccess because you can't know success until you know yourself.

SPEAKER HALL OF FAME. In 2008, Jeffrey was elected by his peers to the National Speaker Association's Speaker Hall of Fame. The designation, CPAE (Counsel of Peers Award for Excellence), honors professional speakers who have reached the top echelon of performance excellence.

ON THE INTERNET. Jeffrey's WOW! websites get more than 100,000 hits per week from readers and seminar attendees. His state-of-the-art presence on the web and e-commerce ability has set the standard among peers, and has won huge praise and acceptance from customers.

TRAINONE ONLINE SALES TRAINING. Award-winning online sales training lessons are available at http://www.trainone.com. The content is pure Jeffrey – fun, pragmatic, real world – and can be immediately implemented. TrainOne's innovation is leading the way in the field of customized e-learning.

AWARD FOR PRESENTATION EXCELLENCE. In 1997, Jeffrey was awarded the designation of Certified Speaking Professional (CSP) by the National Speakers Association. The CSP award has been given fewer than 500 times in the past 25 years and is the association's highest earned award.

ACE OF SALES. The first program that actually helps you make sales! Wanna make more sales, close more deals, AND build loyal relationships? Ace of Sales is the golden ticket of selling and gives you and your people the tools and training to attract, engage, differentiate, thank, stay in touch, and WOW customers. To sign up, visit http://www.aceofsales.com.

SALESBLOG.COM. Understanding the importance of transferring information that's both timely and useful, Jeffrey's Sales Blog adds the ultimate multimedia transfer to Jeffrey's outreach. Log on, subscribe, and stay up to the nanosecond with information to build your sales and success.

RESILIENT LEADER TRAINING. Buy Gitomer and TrainOne have partnered with The Center for Leadership Studies and are now offering a course in *Resilient Leadership*. This dynamic program will test your strengths, expose your vulnerabilities, and reinforce your resilience as a leader and as a person. For more information, call 704/333-1112.

BIG CORPORATE CUSTOMERS. Jeffrey's customers include Coca-Cola, GE, Oracle, US Foodservice, Caterpillar, BMW, Verizon Wireless, CHUBB, MacGregor Golf, Ferguson Enterprises, Kimpton Hotels, Hilton, Enterprise Rent-A-Car, AmeriPride, NCR, Thomson Reuters, Comcast Cable, Raymond James, Liberty Mutual Insurance, Principal Financial Group, Wells Fargo Bank, Monsanto, BlueCross BlueShield, Carlsberg, Wausau Insurance, Northwestern Mutual, MetLife, Sports Authority, GlaxoSmithKline, AC Neilsen, IBM, *The New York Post*, and hundreds of others.

BUYGITOMER
Buy Gitomer, Inc • 704.333.1112
www.gitomer.com

Jeffrey Gitomer's
ACE of SALES™
800.865.7496
www.aceofsales.com

Jeffrey Gitomer's
TRAINONE
TrainOne, Inc • 704.333.8181
www.trainone.com

310 Arlington Avenue, Loft 329 • Charlotte • NC 28203

http://www.facebook.com/JeffreyGitomer

http://www.twitter.com/gitomer

http://www.youtube.com/BuyGitomer

http://www.linkedin.com/in/jeffreygitomer

Other titles by Jeffrey Gitomer

THE LITTLE BOOK OF LEADERSHIP
(Wiley, 2011)

THE LITTLE TEAL BOOK OF TRUST
(FT Press, 2008)

THE SALES BIBLE, NEW EDITION
(HarperCollins, 2008)

THE LITTLE PLATINUM BOOK OF CHA-CHING!
(FT Press, 2007)

THE LITTLE GREEN BOOK OF GETTING YOUR WAY
(FT Press, 2007)

THE LITTLE GOLD BOOK OF YES! ATTITUDE
(FT Press, 2007)

THE LITTLE BLACK BOOK OF CONNECTIONS
(Bard Press, 2006)

THE LITTLE RED BOOK OF SALES ANSWERS
(FT Press, 2006)

THE LITTLE RED BOOK OF SELLING
(Bard Press, 2004)

CUSTOMER SATISFACTION IS WORTHLESS, CUSTOMER LOYALTY IS PRICELESS
(Bard Press, 1998)